The Colonel is a Lady

Beverly Thompson

LT

Book design created by Beverly Thompson

ISBN: 1456308106
ISBN-13: 9781456308100

DEDICATION

I dedicate this book "The Colonel is a Lady" to my wonderful and understanding husband, John Hart Thompson, a 37-year career Navy Captain and Top Gun fighter pilot, and American Airlines Captain who always said, "Get the job done." He taught me with his steadfast encouragement how to fly: to let my creative spirit soar and my soul voice speak.

IN APPRECIATION

The book preparation work spanned several years. Thank you to my editor, Patrick LoBrutto, with additional help from Dr. Lloyd Sampson, and Pat Thibodeau. To the many people about whom this book is written, I want to give my heartfelt thanks and great appreciation for all the time and enthusiastic support you have given me in making this book possible. I have the greatest respect for you, and for all you have contributed to our great country.

The more I delved into Jamie's life, the more reverent I became of her for all she has done for humanity. I am very humbled and honored to relate her story. My desire to write about her began on the day she showed me her scrapbook from her Vietnam days and I said, "Someone should write a book about you." And she replied, "Nobody would be interested in what a little grey-haired lady had to say." And I replied, "Oh, yes, they would. What you did is incredible and someone needs to write a book about you." From that moment on I was committed to writing this book so that the memory of her deeds will not die. Jamie was the driving force behind the foundation of the Vietnam Women's Memorial in Washington, D.C.

The three heroes in the book who served in WWII and Vietnam are authentic and representative of all service men such as the anonymous man in the Vietnam Women's Memorial. Their encounters are fictitious, but their own histories are true. The entire story of Jamie's life is based on fact. She was in each station at every noted time. In writing my book I wanted it to be completely factual, however, I included their fictitious relationships with her in order to emphasize the nature of the horrendous wars waging around her. 1.) Army Air Corp pilot Brad who I portrayed as the love of her life in the New Guinea chapter. 2.) The Marine POW John Boswell in the Philippines and 3.) Marine helicopter pilot Vince in the Vietnam chapter. Everyone else in the book and their experiences are of those who were on the journey with Jamie through her life and are true stories.

FOREWORD

One of the most basic, recurring elements of American history is that safeguarding our freedom at home requires the bravery, resolve and personal sacrifice of American soldiers in far-away lands. War and conflict on a global stage have repeatedly demanded America's full military response, in which thousands upon thousands of young Americans answered the call to duty in all branches of service. Our soldiers in combat have come to know the horrors of war...of destruction and death, and for many, imprisonment.

There are few soldiers closer to the front line of this knowledge than the nurses and doctors in the field...who risk their own lives to save their fellow soldiers.

Evangeline P. Jamison served as a U.S. Army Nurse in World War II, Korea and Vietnam. Jamie retired a Lieutenant Colonel, and the details of her service and recollections of some of the heroes whom she treated are in these pages.

Freedom is not free, and it is difficult sometimes for us to comprehend, much less truly understand and appreciate, how much has been paid for our freedom, our rights and our quality of life in America.

The story of Evangeline Jamison and her service to the country brings to life the detail of individual bravery and sacrifice of our soldiers in war, and the human compassion and caring for our troops that she and the nurses gave.

This is a story of the real cost of our freedom, and a testimony of genuine admiration and gratitude for the soldiers who paid it.

We thank you, Jamie.

Ross Perot

SYNOPSIS OF CHAPTERS

Chapter 1: "We're from Ioway where the tall corn grows." Jamie is growing up, and forming her character for her life ahead. The great Mother heart in such a little girl.

Chapter 2: "Student Nurse" - Meeting fellow student nurses. Agitating to get into the nurse corps at the outbreak of World War II.

Chapter 3: "Brand New Nurse."

Chapter 4: "In the Army Now."

Chapter 5: Basic Training: "Boot Camp in Little Rock, Arkansas" - "We learned to salute, how to pitch a tent and how to find our way back to camp." Duty at Spadra, Santa Barbara, California.

Chapter 6: "Texas Here We Come."

Chapter 7: "Australia"- Treacherous ocean crossing.

Chapter 8: "The Jungles of New Guinea." The war is close. The suicide of a senior nurse profoundly impacted Jamie's thinking. This formed her thoughts about volunteering later for duty in Vietnam to help the nurses as a senior nurse on which they could depend.

Chapter 9: "The Philippines at War's End" - A POW's story, his witnessing of the formation of the "Death March", and his surviving the hell ship and coal mines in Japan as a POW.

Chapter 10: "Ft. Sam Houston, Texas."

Chapter 11: "Back in the Army." Her reasons for getting back in the Army again at Walter Reed Hospital in Washington, D.C.

Chapter 12: "Japan" - during the Korean War. School nurse. Taking the Girl Scouts on a character building adventure in Japan.

Chapter 13: "Letterman Hospital, Calfornia."

Chapter 14: "San Antonio, Texas."

Chapter 15: "Europe." - During the Cold War.

Chapter 16: "Ft. Polk, Louisiana."

Chapter 17: "Vietnam - Arriving in Saigon" - "Although this was my third war, I was shaken at the sight of our fine young wounded who reached the hospital by helicopter, less than an hour after taking fire."

Chapter 18: "Retirement."

Chapter 19: Home: "La Grande Dame" of - and driving force behind the concept and foundation of the Vietnam Women's Memorial. How the memorial came about. Dedication of the Memorial, and "Rolling Thunder" - the men love her.

Chapter 20: "Memorial Debt Retirement."

Chapter 21: "10th Anniversary of the Vietnam Women's Memorial."

Chapter 22: "After Hours." Jamie has her last dance with the love of her life.

The Colonel is a Lady
La Grand Dame of the Vietnam Women's Memorial

✿ ✿ ✿

Beverly Thompson - Author

✿ ✿ ✿

INTRODUCTION

"Arriving in Saigon at 4:30 am in November of 1966 was unsurpassed in sight and sound. The sky was lit by flares and artillery fire and left little doubt we were in the middle of a war zone. There were no hills in Vietnam, only flat land in this area of Vietnam. 'Nam' they called it. You could see for miles. All the time there was action close by, constant mortar attacks. It had a surreal quality. It was foreboding. Danger was always very close at hand.

Young Vietnamese men were sleeping on the base floor at the entrance of the billet where I was taken to spend the next few hours. Later that morning I went by jeep to Long Binh where I was assigned as the Chief Nurse of the 93rd Evacuation Hospital. Although this was my third war I was shaken at the sight of our fine young wounded men who reached the hospital by helicopter, less than an hour after taking fire. It seemed no one had only one wound. Our first task was to find the wounds and treat them appropriately." [Col. Evangeline P. Jamison]

Jamie has been there. She is a little older now with graying hair. This extraordinary woman has a great calmness about her and strength of character and purpose. Her experiences as an Army nurse in three wars and on four continents has forged her like steel. The strife and sacrifices she has endured during her life has not changed her at all. Amazingly she is still as sweet as ever. She is a real life angel who gave her life to and for others.

As I walked into the room, Jamie seemed to be reminiscing about her tour in Vietnam. It was as if all of the scenes passed in review in her mind as she was in the last chapter of life. The tour in Vietnam had been the most horrendous of all her tours in the three wars. She often thought about her experiences as an Army nurse every day of her life.

Jamie sat as she always did when I visited her, with the Vietnam Women's Memorial picture on the wall over her chair. Her smile, like a burst of sunshine, lit the room. Her wonderful smile must have been a great comfort to all when she had served as a nurse. A visit with Jamie was like a tonic. She was marked by simplicity and freedom from artificiality or affectation. How many hundreds of lives have been influenced by her and how many wounded men are alive because of her is not known? She talks softly, but I have learned truly powerful people speak softly, but what they say is profound. Angels speak softly with comforting words of kindness, goodness and love, great love, the highest form of love, love for their fellow man. Do you know what it is like to speak with an angel?

How lucky all those wounded men, women and children were to have Jamie in that place and time to help them. Jamie really is a mother to the world.

✫ ✫ ✫

We met at a Veteran's Day celebration twelve years ago in the small town of Danville, California and were instant friends. I told her I wanted to shake her hand for all she had done for our country, and I mentioned I had served in the Red Cross in Japan, visiting the worst wounded sent there during the Vietnam war. She greeted me by enthusiastically grabbing my face with both her hands along with a quick kiss on my cheek, and said, "Welcome aboard sister! You are also a veteran."

We sat in her office and talked at length about some of our experiences in the hospitals, and I asked her if she ever considered writing a book about her life. She said she didn't have time and was too tired to write a book after working on the Vietnam Women's Memorial for 13 years. She showed me a book of news articles about the Vietnam Women's Memorial and photographs of her tour in Vietnam. She said she hadn't spoken much about the war until 1983. She mentioned these memories of her experiences are with her every day of her life.

Jamie indicated the Vietnam War had been too emotional for most people and no one really wanted to hear about it.

I said, "Jamie we need to write a book about you."

She replied, "Oh honey, why do you want to write a book about me?"

I said, "Because your story needs to be told." I asked her, "What was it like being a nurse in three wars?"

As I asked her, I remembered what one of the patients on a ward in Japan said to me, "You have done so much for me by visiting me, several times a week. How can I ever repay you?" I said to the patient, "Just pass it on."

This is why I'm telling you about Jamie's life - I am passing her story on to you.

CHAPTER 1

We're From Ioway Where The Tall Corn Grows

She spoke softly but with authority and openhearted goodness, and she told me about her life.

The town of Seymour, Iowa was like most pre-World War II small towns. It had huge poplar trees that shaded the road and cast long shadows across the wood frame houses. The total compliment of the town was 1,800. A small town where everyone knew everyone else and everyone's business was news.

It was the age of innocence. People were kind to their neighbors. It was a time and place of good deeds and camaraderie. People were always thinking about the other person, not themselves.

Jamie's mother was kind and sweet. She was about 5' 2" with brown hair and brown eyes that danced when she spoke. She loved music and had been trained at Julliard, which was unusual for this time because most women were homemakers and not involved with a career. She had sung at the opera in Chicago. She was very active in the community in Opera and Drama. Both of Jamie's brothers were very musical also.

Her ancestors left Ireland during the potato famine in 1850, and her father told stories about some of their relatives who had come over to America from Swanlinbar, County Cavan, Ireland which is close to Northern Ireland. She has other relatives that came over from England and their first child born was the first child born on the Mayflower. His name was Perry (Perrigan) White and he was one of Jamie's relatives from her mother's family. John Quincy Adams, the second president of the United States, was also in this family line. Jamie had a wonderful heritage from her family and she carried it with all flags flying throughout her life. A cousin would later remark about her accomplishments. "If Jamie were wounded she would bleed red, white and blue!"

Jamie's father Robert was a big Irishman. Everyone said he was the kindest man in town. He loved everybody. He owned a general store called The Jamison Mercantile Company and he spent long days there.

1

Her family lived above the store in an apartment. Her dad's store was on the square of the town built over a hundred years before, with the park in the center.

Jamie was born in that upstairs bedroom of the apartment in Seymour, Iowa on April 22, 1920. As a baby, Jamie had several bouts with illnesses and her father was very caring. One time he held her as a tiny baby on a pillow all the way to Chicago when she had to see a specialist. Due to pneumonia and was unable to attend first grade, but this setback didn't keep her from excelling in all she did.

✿ ✿ ✿

It was a beautiful sunny day in the little town of Seymour Iowa. Jamie was two and a half years old and barely able to walk. After breakfast she asked her Mother, "Can I take Bert out for a ride in my baby buggy?"

"Yes dear, but remember to take good care of him."

"Oh I will Mommy!" she said and took her dear little brother, who was almost a year old, around the neighborhood in her doll carriage.

The dearest thing in her entire life was her brother Bert. She told everyone, "See my baby? He's my dear baby. I will take care of him. Isn't he beautiful?"

Even as a tiny child she had a big mother heart, a very protective and caring heart. Such a big heart inside such a tiny little girl. If people tried to touch him, she would say. "You can look, but please don't touch my baby. Isn't he beautiful?"

When she was young her mother called her Little Pearl. Her mother's name was Big Pearl, but Jamie didn't like the name Pearl or Little. She would say, "I'm not little!!" So from then on she was called Evangeline.

Jamie's favorite thing to do was to take care of her dear little blond hair, blue eyed brother. There was a bond there that would strengthen over their lifetime. Jamie revered her mother and never objected to any of her rules and regulations. She was always helpful and loyal to all her family.

Jamie learned loyalty early in her life, loyalty to family first, and then loyalty to friends who became family in her future travels and experiences.

One of her earliest memories was when her Dad walked home from town. She loved her father dearly, and would wait for him, screaming, "Daddy, Daddy." She would run to him with her long blond curls flying in the sun, and jump into his arms and he would carry her home. One time she was hiding in a tree and jumped off the branch. He didn't realize she was there, but he saw her and quickly caught her with his big hands.

Jamie was a little bit of a tomboy and was always running with the boys and playing ball with them. Her hair always got snarled, and she would scream when her mother would try to comb it out. She got her hair cut when she was about five years old.

Jamie used to tell people, "We're from Ioway, that's where the tall corn grows." Jamie's Dad had everything for sale in his store. You had to go to Des Moines to find a larger store than his but he lost it in the Depression.

When the Depression started, Jamie was 9 years old. Later she worked at the checkout counter in her father's store, and stocked shelves. Her brother Robert was the butcher. Bert did the ordering. Her father paid the bills. Radios had just become popular, and so, being the enterprising man he was, he opened a radio shop, and sold toasters, irons, etc, which was in 1929, after he went bankrupt. He occasionally took items for trade because the farmers were poor. Jamie and her younger brother Bert sanded an old table her father had taken in and refinished it to look like new. People didn't have all the money they needed. That table had been in someone's milk house, painted red, beige and green. It took all winter to sand it down.

Later he sold Dolen foods out of his store. He employed his three sisters and one brother which made an extended family business. Sunday dinner every week was at either their house or their Grandmother's house. Her father's father had died when he was 10 years old, and the loss made him value his family even more.

Sometimes he loaned money to a friend who needed help. He bought shoes for people who had no shoes, even though he barely had enough to get by. It was a difficult time.

As a young girl Jamie's grandmother was a big influence on Jamie's life and this is probably where she got her patriotism. She used to tell stories about family history, and patriotism, and how her mother had been the first woman to attend a Democratic convention and Jamie's great grandfather was in the Civil War.

When her cousin Elsa and her husband went on a trip to Florida, they asked her, "What would you like us to send you from Florida?" And she said, "An alligator." She always loved animals.

Jamie was surprised to receive a cigar box with the ends cut off, and a little alligator inside. She called the Alligator Jack. Her aunt was worried the alligator hadn't lived through the trip so she sent her another one and they both lived for quite awhile. They didn't grow too much, but she fed them raw liver or hamburger on a toothpick. Her father made cages for her animals and he made a big cage for the alligators with sand in half of it and a big container of water in the other half. She also had rabbits and two dogs.

Her Mother and Uncle realized there weren't many jobs in their town for a young girl who was graduating from high school. She would have to seek a career out of town, and they thought nursing would be a wonderful job for Jamie.

CHAPTER 2

Student Nurse

As soon as Jamie graduated from high school she went into nursing school. Jamie's father paid the tuition, which was $240 for the three-year course. Jamie was all set to embark on her great adventure in life. She was a natural. She loved her brothers and would have defended them with her life if she had had to. Solicitude was her unofficial middle name, because she was always protective and caring.

She was 18 years old, a beautiful young lady and smart. She was also a compassionate, kind and gentle woman. She was slow to anger and quick to forgive. She was now free to do as she wanted and she had wanted to be a nurse for some time. With the impending war, she wanted to serve a purpose greater than herself. She had decided to attend The Presbyterian Hospital for her nurses training.

The Presbyterian Hospital was established in 1883 as a general hospital. It was one of the oldest and one of the best in the entire country.

In 1938, at the time Jamie took her nurses training, Presbyterian Hospital had a capacity of 378 beds. The school of Nursing was organized by the hospital Board of Managers in 1903. Fifteen hundred nurses had graduated from this school by 1938.

The school did not offer preparation in any one specific field of nursing. The school offered special experience in surgical, medical, gynecological, obstetrical and children's nursing. The Nursing School today is a University.

Although students were required to have two years of college to be eligible for enrollment, the school took a small number of girls right out of high school. Jamie was one of those as was her new friend Goldie.

It was mandated by the school that the prospective students have a physical examination, immunization and vaccination. If there were any physical defects they had to be taken care of before admission. Aside from good health, they had to be of good moral character and personality. Jamie had to write a short letter in her own handwriting telling something of her life and occupations she had before her admission to the school. Jamie checked into Sprague Hall and found the rooms fully furnished. The kitchen and dining rooms were all under the supervision of a dietitian. She even inspected the roof and it looked inviting as a place to relax and sun oneself. She met several of the faculty living in the residence. There was also a nurse on duty at all times. She picked up her book for the entire course that cost her $40 and a uniform that cost $75.

On that first day she met Kay, Katherine Marion Rose Meyer, from Lake Linden, Michigan. Kay had a most engaging personality, a good sense of humor and wonderful laugh. Kay and many of their fellow students' friendship stayed with her the rest of her life. Kay was probably her best friend and followed Jamie to New Guinea, Australia, and the Philippines because they were both in the 13th General Hospital Group. They called Kay Teach because she was older than the rest of them, finished college and taught elementary school in an upper Michigan school for two years before becoming a nurse. If anyone had a question they would go to Teach and she would help them.

"Okay Evangeline," Teach said. "If you're going to call me Teach, I'm going to call you Jamie because Evangeline is just too long a name." The name Jamie stuck. Kay would make the Army a career and would eventually retire with the rank of Lieutenant Colonel.

Jamie also met Jean Hayes Smith, or Smitty as they called her, from Rockford, Illinois. She was cute and giggly, and Jamie thought she would probably stay that way because it was her innate personality.

Dorothea Lillian Ernest, Dottie was from Hammond, Indiana. She was her first roommate in the nursing school. She was very quiet. It was Jamie who introduced Dottie to her future husband. He became a doctor and they lived Eureka, South Dakota for the rest of their lives.

Lillian Goldie Dekker was a sweet girl. She was a brunette from Hoopeston, Illinois. Jamie met her when she was 18 years old in nursing school. Goldie was named after her mother's sister who had died at birth.

Rosemary Alice Andreasen was from Hixton, Wisconsin. She had attended La Crosse State Teachers College for three years. She was a big girl. She didn't stand out in the group, but she had a most pleasing personality. They all liked each other from the start.

During Jamie's first quarter of study, her time was devoted to classroom and laboratory work. In her second quarter she spent twelve hours per week in supervised practice on the wards of the Hospital. After six months she had shown all the qualifications of fitness for nursing, good health and had excelled in her studies. She was accepted into full standing in the school and took on more responsibilities in the hospital. She maintained a 48-hour working week and an 8-hour day including her class work. She stood night duty from 11 pm to 7 am some days; then, she would have a short time for rest.

Four weeks vacation was welcome after the long hours of study and duty and there were informal parties or dances and picnics in the summertime. The location of the school afforded many cultural and recreational activities for the nurses.

It had been an age of innocence before war was declared, sweet songs, dreamy romantic movies. The music reflected the mood of the people at the times. Favorites were: *Georgia on My Mind, Baby It's Cold Outside, I Wonder Who's Kissing Her Now, Begin The Beguine, Stompin' at the Savoy, In The Mood* and *Tuxedo Junction*.

In the same year Jamie entered her school of nursing, Irving Berlin had composed the soon to be very popular and patriotic song, *God Bless America*. It was America's unofficial national anthem sung for the first time by Kate Smith on her radio broadcast on Armistice Day 1938. He also introduced his song, *This is the Army*, which became a musical that raised $10 million for the Army Emergency Relief Fund. The musical toured the nation and the world, and was made into a movie starring the young Lt. Ronald Reagan. During World War II, Berlin wrote *This is the Army Mr. Jones, Arms for the Love of America* and he wrote for the Red Cross *Angels of Mercy, There's No business Like Show Business, Easter Parade*, and *White Christmas*. Over the span of his lifetime he would write 900 songs. These songs would help people get through the war.

Jamie and Bert loved going to dance classes together at the YMCA, and danced to all of these popular tunes. Jamie would go to many dances with her new friends at nursing school.

Some of Jamie's studies were Anatomy and Physiology, Bacteriology, Chemistry, Dietetics, Materia Medica, which was a study of drug preparations, their history, their sources and classifications, methods of weighing and measuring, and how they are prescribed. This required an intelligent understanding of mathematics. She also studied Pathology with discussion of all pathological conditions, which cause diseases, and demonstration of pathological conditions at autopsy. There were classes for an introduction to fundamental principles of good nursing, discussions of problems relating to physical and mental care of the patient. Medical Diseases and Medical Nursing was a study of causes and symptoms, prevention and treatment of diseases. Specialized Medical Diseases and

Medical Nursing was a class discussing problems dealing with specialized medical services. She attended lectures by clinicians, recitations and class discussion of vitamins, arthritis, allergies, dermatology and tuberculosis. Surgical Diseases and Surgical Nursing was a study of inflammation, healing of wounds, indications for surgical intervention as regards respiratory, circulatory, musculo-skeletal systems, gastro-intestinal, and pre-operative and post-operative care. She also studied psychology, studying the causes of human conduct in everyday problems with patients and the problems of the sick. She also studied Nervous and Mental Disease, which included discussions of anatomy, and physiology, and pathology of the nervous system. She studied the etiology, symptoms, treatment, preventive measures and good nursing care of the major and minor psychoneuroses.

Other courses were Occupational Therapy, referring to clinical experience working with patients. In the Social Studies classes she studied about adjustment of the student to the school and personnel, and the patient as they related to the hospital and community. The History of Nursing was covered, how nursing evolved from ancient to modern times with emphasis on development of nursing traditions, and many nursing people during that history. Social Problems in Nursing were covered giving the nurses information about patients, the patients' family and significance in the problems of nursing care. Also covered were the different fields of service in nursing open to the graduate nurse, qualifications and problems of each field. A class in Community Health covered the problems in that field including emphasis of the nurse as a teacher of health.

Jamie had decided to become a Neuropsychologist nurse because psychiatric nurses were in short demand when she was in school, and she decided this was the best way she could serve. She knew the other nurses were afraid of this type of nursing, but Jamie was not. She was anxious to get started.

The curriculum schedule was a four-quarter system, which facilitated frequent examinations of the student. It was a three-year course. Half the classes were with medical students.

The school was comprised of a nursing arts laboratory, library, an alumnae room and offices for instructors, a dining room and a newly constructed cafeteria.

The general hospital unit of service in the event of war was organized as originally ordered by the Surgeon General of the U.S. Army. This consisted of a staff of twenty-eight physicians and four laboratory scientists. This had been upgraded to include surgical staff and medical staff of forty-eight and a lab staff of seven.

A Miss Emma Aylward was the matron of the nurse's residence, which was the eight-story Sprague Hall. She had been there since the founding of the school in 1903. During the time Jamie was in school 10 members of the nursing staff resigned and joined the U.S. Army Nurse Corps.

At Presbyterian hospital many of the staff were doing research and doing studies of medical problems at the same time they were teaching. This afforded the very best in providing the latest information in nursing to the student nurses.

Her older brother Robert had always been generous to her when she was in nursing school. He always put $10 in the letters every time he wrote to her.

Jamie's nurse friends received their diplomas in the fall of 1941.

CHAPTER 3

Brand New Nurse

Jamie received her diploma April 10, 1942 at graduation ceremonies at 4th Presbyterian Church in Chicago. Her entire family was there when Jamie became a brand new nurse. When nurses were pinned, they had by tradition taken off their black shoes and black hose, and put on white shoes and white nylons to signify they were now nurses.

In 1941, her brother Bert was in an auto accident when he was in college at Parsons Presbyterian College in South Iowa. He had just sung in an a cappella choir, and was driving home in the rain and he went off the road. He sustained nine injuries and dropped out of school for the rest of the semester. The Army didn't want him, and he was very disappointed. Her dear brother whom she used to put in her doll carriage when he was a baby, had grown to be a very handsome skinny young man with blond hair and blue eyes. Jamie had hazel eyes and brown hair and was not so skinny.

When Jamie went to homecoming at the University of Illinois, Bert said, "I'm coming to Chicago next week to join the Navy."

Jamie said, "What makes you think the Navy wants you if the Army won't take you?" But he came to Chicago and they accepted him. Now she had two brothers in the Navy, and so she was more and more insistent on being called.

Bert was on a tanker. It was like a carrier that refueled the rest of the fleet. Her older brother was 10 years older than she, and was a Seabee. He would eventually become a Navy Chief.

After Pearl Harbor was bombed, all Jamie could think about was getting into the Army NOW. She first read about the attack on Pearl Harbor in the newspaper. The entire nation was in shock. The entire nation went into high gear to do everything they could. Everyone was behind the war effort. It was a united front and everyone wanted to do their part to help out. This was a war for freedom and to keep democracy alive in the world.

Jamie was a part of The Greatest Generation. Sometimes greatness and leadership are inherent in a person. Or perhaps it comes from a divine being, or it's the synapses formed long ago by one's forbearers, or it comes in a dream ... maybe it's just unexplainable. But it's definitely a calling. Whatever it was in Jamie's case, it was an overwhelming calling to become a nurse and help her fellow man. It's called Agape (from the Greek word for unselfish love). She was becoming a part of a cause greater than herself. Jamie was a super patriot, one of the women who went the extra mile and joined the service to serve their country, and put their lives on the line.

Jamie moved in with four of her student classmates. Kay, who was her best friend, Smitty, Rosemary and Goldie. It was a Sisterhood.

She and three of her friends were staying in a room with a Murphy bed, and three regular beds.

Of course Jamie's classmates couldn't wait to sign their names and go on active duty. But the problem was the Army didn't call them. So that summer as a student nurse she took a job on board the S.S. Alabama and went to Sault Ste. Marie and back to Pouton & Hancock in Michigan, and back for the 5 day trip while waiting to be called into the Army. She was on that job for a month or so. Then, she started doing private duty.

Just before she went into the Army, her younger brother Bert and she shared an apartment for about a year.

Her older brother Robert was working in Washington State. He helped build the Grand Coolie Dam. He also helped to build Fort Rosecrans in San Diego.

Jamie said to her friends, "I don't know if I should go home for Christmas or buy a new coat. I certainly need one!" When she was a student nurse, she had no money so she didn't buy the coat, but she did go home.

Jamie was a stand-out person, a natural leader, and she wanted to get on with her life as a nurse. One day she said to the girls, "You know this waiting is getting on my nerves. When Christmas vacation is over, I'm going down to Army Headquarters and tell them to call me to active duty, send me any place they want to, but recall me when they re-activate the unit." Her classmates said, "Well Jamie if you're going to do it, we're going to do it." So the four of them, Rosemary Andreason, Jean Hays Smith, Katherine Marion Rose Meyer and Jamie, went to the 6th Army headquarters in Chicago. She was a woman on a mission. She called the Army daily, and finally they said, "All right come on in." So before they knew it, they were sent to their first duty station.

CHAPTER 4

In The Army Now

Jamie could not believe the exalted feeling she felt when finally inducted into the Army on February 3, 1943 as a Reserve Nurse in the Army Nurse Corps, with the rank of 2nd Lieutenant. Her Oath Of Office was administered to her by a civil officer in Chicago Illinois, and it read: I, Evangeline P. Jamison having been appointed a Reserve Nurse, Army Nurse Corps, in the Regular Army of the United States, do solemnly swear that I will support and defend the Constitution of the United States against all enemies, foreign and domestic; that I will bear true faith and allegiance to the same; that I take this obligation freely, without any mental reservation or purpose of evasion; and that I will well and faithfully discharge the duties of the office upon which I am about to enter: So help me God. These vows were not taken lightly by Jamie to which her life would attest. She had a firm resolve to do her very best as a nurse in the Army. One of the greatest things about Jamie was the fact she could never let someone down if they needed help. There are few people in the world who are genuinely concerned about their brother; Jamie was one of the few.

Her life really and truly began at this moment. She was in the Army now and no matter what, she was duty bound to do her very best. Her formative years would serve her well; instilled in her were the stories her grandmother told her about patriotism, and doing one's duty for your country. Her grandmother told her about all the great people who had formed our great country, many with great sacrifice. She also explained about her own forbearers who came over to this country on the Mayflower. Her forbearers were some of the first Europeans to set foot in this great land. Many of her relatives were patriots in the Revolutionary war. Her grandmother instilled in Jamie the possibility of one person doing a lot of good, and making a difference.

A World War I hospital reactivated for World War II became their training school. The government reorganized this 13th General Hospital and most of the people who comprised this group of doctors and nurses were friends from the Presbyterian Hospital. A lot of the doctors had taught them, and a lot of them had taught at Rush Medical School where they had many classes. The unit was not activated right away.

Jamie was very self-confident. She was young and inexperienced as a nurse, but she had had excellent training at the best nursing school in the country and she was prepared for her new duty station. Her confidence would grow as she put her knowledge of nursing to the test with her patients. She was eager to get on with the program and with her friends. They were full of life and seeking adventure as they went to their first duty station.

She was going to defend her country in any way she could and be there for the fighting men when they were wounded. This was her mission. It was a fight to the end to keep freedom alive. It was all very clear to everyone who the enemy was and what they were about. There was a unified force working together to right the wrongs that had been created by greedy, sadistic and cruel men. It was a war of good against evil. These were frightening and uneasy times.

Women were coming of age in the war effort. They were filling the ranks quickly. The government realized if we were going to win this war, they had to enlist a lot of women into the work force to replace the men who had gone to war, and there were a lot of propaganda posters reminding the women their men needed their support here at home. A lot of women wanted to be independent, were patriotic, and wanted a little economic relief after the Depression years; however, there was a lot of discrimination in the workplace and a lot of confusion about woman's place in society because the husband had always been the head of the household. Many women worked long hours with only half the pay as the men, even though they were doing the same work.

For the woman at home shortages of food, clothing and gasoline made it difficult to maintain duties as a wife and homemaker. Victory gardens sprang up and growing fresh produce provided food for the table. Sugar was rationed because it was used to make gunpowder. Materials like silk, nylon and cotton were used to make military clothing and parachutes. People turned in rubber tires and metal. Gasoline was rationed and everyone had a ration card. People sacrificed and did all they could for the war effort.

Like the famous Rosie the Riveter, women worked at defense plants and worked with machinery, making tanks and planes. It was an era of mass production. They even ferried planes to different destinations freeing up the men so they could fight in the war.

Jamie was unaware of any prejudice against her or other women. All she cared about was patients and her nurses and whether she were giving them the best of care.

In 1942 the Women's Army Auxiliary Corps was founded. 60,000 women joined the ranks within a year of the buildup. Congress was so impressed with these women the Women's Army Corps was changed from Auxiliary Corps to full military status. By 1944 the Corps number had reached 100,000.

Jamie's brothers were shocked she had joined the Army. Jamie very proudly said to them, "Well I'm a woman and I'm in the Army now."

It was very difficult for Jamie's mother to part with the children she loved so dearly, to see them all go off to war. All three of them would be sent to the Pacific. Her mother said, "What am I going to do when you all leave?" Jamie said, "Go back to Iowa and take care of my father and crochet a tablecloth for me." Her mother wrote to her three children every day with carbon copies to all.

Jamie was so pleased her cousins, David James and Louie and their parents came to the train to see her off when she left on her trip to Little Rock Arkansas and Basic Training. They had brought a corsage for her. Of course, Army personnel weren't supposed to have corsages on their uniforms, but she wore it anyway.

CHAPTER 5

Basic Training in Little Rock, Arkansas

The Army sent Jamie and her friends to Camp Joseph T. Robinson for basic training along with all the Army enlisted men and all the doctors, corpsmen, and nurses. They were there six weeks in Little Rock, Arkansas. This was their orientation to Army nursing. All newly commissioned nurses learned about Army customs, organization, defense tactics, personnel administration and property responsibility. They also filled out a lot of forms. They learned how to administer anesthesia, oxygen therapy and how to prevent and treat shock. Psychiatric nurses were in high demand and they learned how to medicate patients. Uniforms were ordered, they went through a physical exam and had shots for typhoid, typhus and smallpox. Then, the rigorous training began. In six weeks they learned Army protocol, how to suture wounds, survive a simulated enemy attack and how to march. They did calisthenics and ran to get the adrenalin going. It was challenging work, but so necessary. They learned to salute, to pitch a tent and spit-shine their boots.

To spit-shine one's boot the Army way, you need a can of Kiwi boot polish, a cloth and a cigarette lighter. Each night for five nights you use some boot polish and spread it over the boot, then burn the polish into the boot leather with the cigarette lighter and buff it until you got a high gloss with the soft cloth.

They equipped these raw recruits with flashlights, goggles, helmets, and heavy gear. They took them out about five miles in a covered truck, then gave them a compass, canteen of water, a small mess pack, a first aid kit, and a grid map and said, "Find your way back to camp." They were a group of six soldiers, two males and four females. They were on their own. After some reconnoitering with the compass they were on their way. They saw jackrabbits, armadillos, and red foxes and tried to stay far away from the rattlesnakes. The heat was relentless, and they bogged down several times from the weight of their backpacks. They had almost used up all the water in their canteens when they finally made their way back to camp. They were exhausted and they had used leg and back muscles they hadn't used before. This was good training because the Army wanted tough and resilient women and men, for all the things they would face at future duty stations.

After dinner in the chow hall they repaired to bed for much needed rest. Next morning they were up at 5 am, standing at attention for roll call in their crisp uniforms with spit shined boots for inspection in front of the Drill Master.

Then they were taught how to debark on a ship down a rope ladder. Later, in New Guinea, when they went down a rope ladder off the side of a ship, they were thankful they were taught how to do this. When they were through at the six-week basic training, they were ready for their first assignment and equipped with knowledge that would stand them in good stead for all of their tours. Goldie met her future husband Fred at Camp Robinson.

CHAPTER 6

Texas Here We Come

They were all part of the 13th Hospital Group and Jamie was a brand new 2nd Lieutenant. On the 3rd of February 1942, they trooped down to Longview, Texas to Army General Hospital, which was a 1,000 bed brand new hospital. The four of them made up the station complement, along with the nine nurses who had arrived with them, thirteen altogether, but no patients, so every day they would tackle another ward getting it ready, shampooing the floors, cleaning the beds, etc. Jamie ordered all the equipment they needed. It was new to her, but she learned fast.

There were Cajuns and Mexicans later who helped out. They were wearing their first pair of shoes when they came on base. It was interesting to her to see these families come through the gate in jalopies or trailers. It was unreal to her because she had come from Chicago.

The nurses were thrilled to be sent to their first duty station together, and took great comfort in knowing they would always be together as a unit. They didn't know at the time they would form life long friendships with each other. The bonding of the nurses was similar to the bonding of the men in war - that of life and death experiences and depending on each other through everything.

✿ ✿ ✿

Next they were sent to Spadra, in Southern California, which was a desert training center. You can't find it on the map now, but it was near Pomona, and out in the middle of nowhere. The Kellogg Horse Ranch was close by and Jamie saw these horses and took pictures of them. One horse had belonged to Rudolph Valentino.

Spadra was kind of a makeshift place. They were in an old Wally Reed narcotic hospital. That's where the permanent buildings were and that was where nurses were housed. The Army Corps of Engineers built temporary units for the hospitals, and the male officers and enlisted men lived in tents. The nurses had all the injuries from the desert command to administer. It got over 100 degrees during the day, and it was also very hot at night.

Jamie assisted in the organization of the Neuropsychiatric wards. She supervised the nurses and enlisted personnel. She accounted for patients at all times in records and reports that were, and would be, excellent.

For relaxation, there wasn't much to do at this remote encampment, so they listened to the radio at night. They were all very relieved when they got orders to Hoff General in Santa Barbara. They had a very short stint there also.

When the exercises ended, Goldie was sent to the 9th Service Command in Brigham, Utah. The hospital there was filled with nurses and Goldie was then sent to Camp Adair, Oregon and from there she went to Camp Beale, California. At that point, all the nurses came to Pittsburg, California.

Jamie had been sent TDY, which is temporary duty, for four months to Hoff General in Santa Barbara and the 42nd General Hospital, on September 18, 1943. She was assigned as a psychiatric nurse and did exemplary work. She also organized and equipped the Neuropsychiatric wards as the ward's new Supervisor. She had night duty, working 8 to 12 wards, with 12-hour shifts. Jamie worked 7 a.m. - 7 p.m. She had 8 or 10 wards to work the Psychiatric Section as a new nurse. She had corpsmen to help out and they were always good to the nurses.

✿ ✿ ✿

Jamie was sent to Pittsburg, California. Pittsburg is about 20 miles inland from San Francisco. It was the departure point for all the ships leaving from the west coast to the war. Jamie was only at Pittsburg for a very short time. Her younger brother was at Camp Parks at that time, near Dublin. He was privy to a memo about who was arriving and departing, and he found out Jamie was stationed there and he came out to see her. They had a nice day together. Before she knew it, she was on her way to Australia.

CHAPTER 7

Australia

The sky was overcast and there was an ominous mood in the air even before the nurses boarded the Dutch ship, New Amsterdam for Australia on January 5, 1944. They arrived in their destination January 22, 1944. The ship had been a luxury liner and had been made into a troop ship. Later, Jamie would exclaim to her nurse friends, "They sure took their time getting there." It took 17 days from San Francisco to Sydney. The ship set out with 200 excited nurses going to do their part for the war effort.

They had all settled in their quarters, which were not very elegant. They had 8 to 10 people to a large room and they slept in bunk beds. Jamie, being a bit of a tomboy, and in great physical condition had climbed up into the top bunk and declared this was her bed.

It was difficult to sleep much of the night with the temperatures between 90 and 100 degrees. The metal of the ship made it even hotter. The girls longed to get back on firm land and start their mission to the wounded. It was comforting to have her three good friends with her, the little band of nurses going out into the world, to unchartered waters half way across the world. Jamie thought about the early years of her life and her thoughts also centered on how very important America was to her. She was very close to her Mother and Father and missed them very much. Her brothers were very special to her too, they had a strong bond and she would have defended them with her life if she had to. On that first night on board, she was finally lulled to sleep by the water slapping up against the side of the ship.

The nurses were dressed in their woolen uniforms. When they left the United States it was January and they were dressed in uniforms that were a brown/green wool cloth during the day, and they were soaked with sweat from the 90 to 100 degree temperatures.

It was a high adventure going to a foreign land, but extremely dangerous because there were Japanese and German submarines in the murky waters waiting for a strike on a ship. The ship was surrounded by a combatant group of ships - a sonar ship, and destroyers to protect the fleet of ships in the convoy. All ships by pre-arranged plans did a zigzag evasion tactic in unison across the Pacific. It was a slow trip but a little safer. The method of shooting the stars and planets was done by using a sextant to get a fix on an object or destination. The ships' navigation equipment was sketchy at best. Sometimes they could pick up a bogey or enemy plane hundreds of miles away and other times they got no message until they were right on them. They stopped zigzagging every now and then when visibility was bad, putting them in an even more vulnerable position.

The nurses were full of adventure but had a nagging apprehension about the trip. They lived in such uncertain times then. The war was close, and they were not free most of the time to come and go as they chose on the ship. They had roll call daily to make sure everyone was accounted for, but there was no military regimen for the nurses because they were not a part of ship's company.

Several times in the crossing they had a quiet time when they couldn't speak because a submarine had been detected on the sonar screen. These were tense times. You could cut the tension with a knife. The moments eked slowly by. The girls had heard stories of ships being blown up and men lost at sea. It had turned into a rough crossing. Jamie tried to put the possibility of something like that happening out of her mind.

The nurses were a talkative group and hailed from all over the country but mostly they were from the Midwest farms and so were, for the most part, country girls. They were selfless young women who had very high ideals.

There was a lot of talk about the new duty station. They wondered what the new duty station would be like and if they would all be together.

There wasn't much to do on deck but watch a movie or play cards. The girls were resourceful and found a little card table for their games. They played dominoes and they spent days playing canasta, with the perfect foursome for cards; Jamie won most of the time. One of Jamie's friends taught her how to knit a blanket to help pass the time.

✫ ✫ ✫

When Jamie set foot on land at Sydney, Australia, January 1944, the first thing she did was ask, "Have you got a drink of water? It's hotter than hell here!" That was the hottest day of the year and they were still dressed in their woolen uniforms.

Soon they were taken to the base. The base was called The Punchbowl. Quarters were nice at their base camp, because they were assigned to a base hospital outside of Sydney. They had a bed and a mattress and the pillows they had brought from home.

They reported to the hospital and did their daily chores. There weren't many bloody or freshly wounded men because the war was not too close. Some of the men got looking very grubby with their long hair and Jamie took pity on them. She couldn't stand it any more and started cutting their hair.

When the nurses had some time off they went to Brisbane and enjoyed the city. The vast interior of Australia is a huge inhospitable continent with more land than people, but the cities are small enclaves of humanity situated along the coast. The towns were throwbacks to the 20's and the people were happy that way. They frequently went to the milk bars which were like American ice cream shops..

The Australians loved the old ways and Jamie didn't see many flashy new cars or extravagant homes. These people were good homey people on the farm, in a land just beginning to enter the world of manufacturing. The Australians were basically Irish and English peoples and racially very exclusive. Not many Asians were living in the country, and now that the war had begun Australia was totally allied with the United States in the war effort.

General Douglas MacArthur arrived in Australia in March of 1942 with his wife and young son. He was brilliant and reserved and aloof. He was arrogant with an indomitable self-confidence instilled in him by his father, strong willed mother, and West Point. His mother had molded him for greatness and he would follow in his father's footsteps. His father was General Arthur MacArthur who had fought in the Spanish American war in the Philippines and helped win it as a United States possession. MacArthur's father had instilled in his son a sense of loyalty to the Filipinos as an American Trust and he was the guardian of that trust.

On December 8, 1941 the Japanese had attacked the Philippines smashing General MacArthur's inept defenses and he retreated to Corregidor. He struggled to hold onto this island but food and armaments were in short supply, and although promises from Washington came, eventually he could not organize a good defense against the enemy. On March 12th, General McArthur left the Philippines, vowing to return, and was sent by President Roosevelt to Australia where he was to become

Supreme Commander of the United Nations forces in the Pacific. Jamie saw him occasionally but not in a work situation.

A group of 30 doctors and nurses bought a horse, saddle and bridle from a mess Sergeant for $200. They sold the horse later on to another mess sergeant for the same price. They had him for five months. They rented a place for the horse from a farmer. At 3:30 they were off duty, and would saddle up and ride to the top of a 3,000 foot mountain to watch the lights go on in Sydney. There were no blackouts then, those were only in the States. They would stop to buy a bottle of Australian beer, which was 22% alcohol, buy half a barbequed chicken and eat the chicken and drink the beer.

Then they got home at dusk. They each had a cot, a potbelly stove and folding chairs and so they sat on the floor a lot and toasted marshmallows. They'd put on a pot of coffee with water and eggshells and sit and talk about men or anything that came to a young woman's mind.

Harry was a handsome brunette tall, and sort of shy. Jamie met him in the Officer's club and soon they were dating. When they were off at 3:30 they used to saddle up their horses and go for long rides in the countryside on beautiful sunny days. Each was trying to impress the other. Jamie loved horses, and showed off her riding skills riding around in the ring on a high stepping horse. After she had gotten the horse warmed up in the ring, she said, "Let's go on a trail ride."

Harry could not get his horse to move and so the stable hand got on and whipped the reluctant horse into a fine frenzy, and then said to Harry "Okay, get on." Harry got on the horse and the horse took off and was gone over the horizon like the speed of lightning. Eventually he came back. Not so much the worse for wear, but a little embarrassed. He was not a horseman and had been doing well just to stay on the horse on the wild ride.

Another day would be a swimming day where he could show off his swimming skills to Jamie, swimming out to a barge in the lagoon. It was pleasant. They laughed and tossed water at each other and talked about their lives and dreams as young people who think they are in love.

The romance was called short because after Jamie's six-month tour of duty was over in Australia, she was being sent to New Guinea.

In 1942 the Japanese had resumed major attacks at Bataan. On May 30, 1942 they bombed Sydney, Australia. On June 7, the Japanese bombed Newcastle.

On March 7th, 1942 the Japanese had landed in East New Guinea. In 1942 there had been many attacks on Lae in New Guinea, which was about

40 miles from Finschhafen, which gave the Australian pilots experience and also boosted morale, but the Japanese were not deterred. They planned on invading Port Moresby in New Guinea. After dark on July 21, 1942, the Japanese landed in Papua, New Guinea on the northern coast. It was a fairly large invasion force. The next day, Allied troops tried to stave off their invasion but through a mist, the enemy moved silently into the jungle. Their objective was Port Moresby, about 70 miles over narrow jungle trails with overgrown moss with sheer drop-offs into mountain streams up into 13,000 foot mountains. General MacArthur alerted the small reconnaissance unit to protect the area. A small Company was sent in the only plane capable of landing on the small airstrip in Komodo. Half way to Port Moresby, the Australians clashed with the Japanese. Outnumbered, and without proper weapons the Australians retreated and the airfield was secured by the Japanese. On Sept 5, they had made it to the village just before Port Moresby fell but their men were out of rations, sick, and no reinforcements were forthcoming. They were bombed and strafed by the 5th Air Force. The fight was fierce. The allies re-secured the air base at Komodo, and then retreated back to where they had landed and to Buna-Gonna. The Japanese were camouflaged by the jungle and it was difficult to pinpoint their locations in a driving rainstorm. The Allies became bogged down in mud.

The Japanese had also landed at Milne bay about 300 miles to the East of Port Moresby at the tip of New Guinea. They were met with superior force both on land and from the air to protect the base there. However, some of the weapons were inoperable because of jungle mold that had grown in them. After the superior assault by allied forces, the Japanese were soon on the run to the beach and quickly into their ships and evacuated the area. This was the Allies first big victory over the Japanese.

In January of 1943, the United States and Australian troops joined forces in New Guinea. In May, as the battle was shaping up, Admiral Inoue at Rabaul was in charge of the Port Moresby invasion. But he postponed the invasion until the US carriers could be taken care of and the invasion never took place. Japan's aura of invincibility had been badly shaken. In December of that year, US forces invaded New Britain Island in North New Guinea.

✯ ✯ ✯

Prior to Jamie's arrival at Finschhafen, General MacArthur had ordered an amphibious attack on Finschhafen, which was a minor port located on the eastern side of the Huon Peninsula, occupied by and used by the Japanese for barge traffic. There were 5,000 Japanese occupying Finschhafen at the time. Many approaches to Finschhafen had to be cleared of the enemy before this attack. Other troops moved north from Nadzab to get the Japanese on the run until they encountered dense bamboo forests and sheer cliffs at 6,500 feet. The Australians moved into valleys near Finschhafen to secure more forward air bases. Lae was captured, and Dumpu where an airstrip was constructed. Support for the troops during this action depended on the conversion of airfields that could handle troop aircraft. The Japanese General Nakai, disturbed by the loss of Finschhafen after some ferocious battles, stationed his force in the Huon Peninsula to recapture Finschhafen, leaving only a small contingent to defend the base area. Major Yamada, commanding Finschhafen, judged the town would be the next target. He placed most of his troops south and west of the town leaving few at its northern side. The landings on LCIs and LSTs of the Australians took place at night on the narrow coastal strip at Scarlet beach. Yamada's troops were destroyed there. The Australians took Finschaffen after many battles.

These battles are a brief microcosm of many battles for New Guinea.

With the capture of Finschhafen, and the area secured, the Allies had control of anchorages from Lae to Scarlet Beach. Construction crews repaired the runway to a 5,000-foot runway at Finschhafen. Harbor dredging began and a floating dock installed and buildings were constructed. An important base was under construction.

CHAPTER 8

The Jungles of New Guinea

All the doctors and nurses at the hospital in Australia were ordered to go to New Guinea to care for the wounded because they didn't have enough men to finish the hospital there. The doctors along with the nurses learned how to construct a hospital in a hurry. This new base was closer to the pickup point for patients to be brought into the hospital. So they were on the move again. Jamie was reluctant to go, but she had to do her duty.

New Guinea was of paramount importance to the Australians, and as President Woodrow Wilson had advised in 1919, the Japanese should not be allowed to control the island. If it had in 1942, the Japanese would quite possibly have taken over Australia.

New Guinea was thought of as paradise in the South Pacific. A beautiful place, it had tall volcanic hills, teeming jungles and ethereal mists that rise in the early mornings. You can't escape the grandeur of the place, but it was war torn when Jamie got there.

They arrived in Nora Bay on July 10, 1944. Jamie and the other nurses would be serving at an Army hospital on Finschhafen with the 13th General Hospital, which was a Navy base. The heat was oppressive, one could hardly breathe. As the nurses could see from the ship, there was a lot of activity in the harbor, with small boats going about and men working to build buildings for this forward base. The ship dropped anchor off shore, and they were ordered over the side of the ship and down the rope ladder. Not very ladylike. Even with all their training, it was a little unnerving as the ship was so high. They had to get a really firm grip on the ropes because it was a long way down into the water. The local native women paddled out to greet the ship in their long carved out canoes bearing fruit and leis for all. It was a noisy affair with the men shouting and whistling, and making wolf calls to the girls.

Jamie said to Smitty as they were going over the side, "Boy, I'm sure glad we had all that training or we'd be in duck soup right now." It was a mad scramble with 100 nurses going over the side. Several small Navy landing crafts, called LCPs, pulled up by the side of the ship to take them to the beach.

When their feet touched dry land, it felt so good. It took awhile for them to get their land legs but it was good to be on firm land again. It had taken only one week to sail to New Guinea from Australia, but it had seemed like an eternity because it had been so stressful with the war all around them.

As they boarded a truck, there was dust flying from the jeeps racing around them. There were people rushing in every direction carrying boxes of medical and armament supplies from the ships, loading some supplies onto other ships. They knew what their jobs were and they carried them out efficiently, but when they saw the nurses they dropped everything and came to get a closer look.

There were hundreds of troops lining the side of the road for 18 miles to where they would household them at Finschhafen. They were cheering wildly because they hadn't seen an American woman for so long. The noise was almost unbearable. As they went in the truck in the midst of the cheering and wolf calling men a certain Lieutenant was watching them. His eye caught a beautiful brunette, and his eyes followed her as she went by him, and he knew it was kismet. In his eyes she was the most beautiful woman he had ever seen. She carried herself with an old world presence. He would wait for just the right moment to seek her out after all the excitement of the day had subsided, to get acquainted with her.

The jungle was hot and oppressive as they wound their way up the hill to the stone steps to their quarters. The ocean, sun-swept beaches, tropical breezes and lazy palm trees were very tranquil, but not too far away the war was in full force. That evening, after they settled into their new home, the troops came over to see if there were anyone from their hometown and to get acquainted.

Jamie's billet in New Guinea was to be for 13 months and there was a lot of work to be done in that short time. They were living in a jungle and there was no relief from the heat. Japanese troops were on the other side of the island.

They got settled in their metal roofed buildings called Quonset huts; they were like dormitories. Her building had four nurses in it. They had a makeshift shower with curtains and a pot of water that could be released to pour over themselves outside. Occasionally pilots would fly low over the showers for a closer look.

The nurses lived in fenced in quarters with armed guards standing watch around the clock. When they left their quarters they were always accompanied by the armed guards. There was also a curfew. No one was to be out after dark. Two armed guards accompanied the nurses if they traveled off the post outside the fence. There were enemy guerilla groups roaming the area and the Army wanted their nurses sheltered.

The evening was cool and on that first night Jamie could see the horizon just as the sun was setting and that split second white/green flash as the sun sank below the horizon. This reminded her of the symbol of the Japanese military machine and their flag of the rising sun. She wondered if it was a rising sun or would it be a setting sun. It was an all out effort to keep democracy afloat in a sea of uncertainty.

That first night the nurses undressed in front of everybody else, and Jamie joked, "Close your eyes if you don't want to see anything." When they went to bed they listened to a wireless radio and were just about asleep when something started hitting their roof in rapid succession. They thought they were under attack and ran outside. What a relief to know it was just cocoanuts!

Morning came early and all nurses reported to the hospital where they were introduced to the doctors and given assignments. Quickly, a daily routine was established. They were issued brown and white seersucker dresses to wear instead of fatigues. They looked pretty feminine in New Guinea.

The camp was not large. It had a mess hall, a barracks for operations, and the hospital and an ammo dump, a runway and several small planes.

Jamie made her daily rounds on the wards. Her duties were as Charge Nurse of the ward and later as supervisor of the Neuropsychiatric section. She instructed nurses and corpsmen in their special duties and procedures in the Neuropsychiatric wards. She gave intravenous sedations, sedative packs, sedative tubs and supervised the personal hygiene care of patients. She administered sulfa drugs and treated tropical diseases, and dehydration.

After her rounds were made, she helped to build the rest of the hospital. The hospital was half finished, but everyone worked hard to make it habitable. Doctors and nurses and corpsmen worked side by side.

At Finschhafen, the casualties were all fresh wounds. Most of the POW's were sent to them from the Philippines, and, after they were treated they were sent to Australia. There were a lot of cases of malaria, typhus, dysentery, diphtheria, leprosy and bubonic plague. The nurses were not skilled in these diseases but did the best they could to help the patients heal.

A lot of the patients had shell-shock or battle fatigue and had to be treated for that. This was a result of experiencing a horrific and life threatening trauma. This experience left these patients suffering flashbacks where they relived the trauma, possibly permanently changing the brain's chemical sensitivity. Nightmares, anxiety, fatigue, lack of sleep, depression, shaking, confusion, memory loss and anger outbursts were also symptoms.

These symptoms could arise at any time. Some might not occur for years. Some of the effects of too much stress damages the heart and raises the blood pressure and this can lead to digestive problems. It is very damaging to the brain resulting in brain aging and impaired cognitive responses.

When the body is faced with a stressful situation, the adrenaline is released in the body for quick energy to the muscles and a fight or flight response, releasing stress hormones, which electrify the hippocampus - the part of the brain that controls memory so you can deal with a situation when it occurs again. This is why people can remember vividly when these horrible stressful scenes occurred. But when this scenario is repeated again and again the body responses decline, as the memory and physical problems occur. In some cases, prolonged exposure to this stress can injure hippocampus brain cells and with lack of oxygen, the patient can die or it can cause a stroke. The patients were treated with Psychotherapy and medication. The nurses treated the patients in behavioral therapy that included breathing therapy.

Being a Big Ear was the most helpful. The nurses helped them expose the harmful thoughts by talking with them to help them relive some of their fears, and help them modify their thinking process to eliminate the stressful negative thoughts and memories.

They changed their patient's diets, serving them wholesome food and kept their diets free of coffee or tea. Proper sleep helped, as well as exercise, or by sitting in a chair quietly, like in a yoga meditation, in a state of muscle relaxation, to keep from being distracted by anything and this required discipline and great effort in some cases.

Some had bad reactions to the horrific events and some didn't have any bad effects. The worse the tragedy, the more probability it was to be a bad reaction. These men needed to be protected from further exposure to these traumatic events. Jamie handled the patients tactfully and very well. She had great potential ability as a nurse, but did not yet have the maturity of judgment required to be a Chief Psychiatric nurse. Rather rudimentary care was given the patients.

The hospital was by the ocean, but the nurses didn't swim because the water from the ships had dirtied it. There were battleships and smaller craft in the harbor with many small boats going back and forth taking people to and from the ship that lay docked there. Large supply ships came in from time to time with much needed surgical supplies, and other hospital supplies.

The nurses loved to see the ships come in because the Navy men would invite them to dinner on the ships. They served real meat and fresh fruit on the ships, so it was a treat. Otherwise, they had their daily portions of corned beef and Spam, beef jerky, fruit cocktail and powdered milk as a daily ration. Jamie used to make powdered milk for her patients to drink. She also produced food for the patients because the government only sent canned food. She enjoyed New Guinea. Her Mom sent garden seeds. Most of the land was sand, but she planted radishes and lettuce and vegetables and they thrived. Smitty once asked her, "Why do you have to plant all those vegetables?" and Jamie answered, "I had to do something – because I'm a country girl." She formed strong alliances with the other nurses. It was a bond that would last for years, not to be broken. They were family!

On her first ride in a jeep, the guard tossed his pistol on the seat where she was sitting and told her to hold onto it. This was the only time she would ever hold a weapon. The enemy was very close and the nurses had to be protected by the guards.

Some of the Army Air Corps pilots would fly in from other bases close to their base and sometimes the girls would get a flight to the Philippines by trading their beer with the pilots. The beer was good. It was 18% alcohol but Jamie never remembered drinking a lot. She really didn't like the stuff but it was so hot there and a beer tasted good sometimes.

She would say, Okay when someone would ask her out for a date, but she would forget whom she had said she would date. She got into a problem with all the gentlemen who wanted to date her when they would all show up at once. Soon she kept a datebook to keep things straight. They were coming to her boarding place to see them, so Jamie had to set up a table to take down names and if anyone wanted to see Mary Jones or Suzy Jones, someone would have to go out to find her. They were glad to see the nurses but the nurses were just as glad to see them because that was what they went to New Guinea for, to see them and take care of them.

✡ ✡ ✡

Brad, the handsome young Captain in the Army Air Corps who had spotted Jamie the day she had arrived in New Guinea, came to visit her. Brad was stationed down the road at Nadzab. When Jamie and Brad's eyes met, they somehow knew they had been together in a past life. It was love at first sight. Tom had come with Brad and Smitty met Tom at the same time.

Before long, Jamie and Smitty, her dear friend, did a lot of double dating with these two gentlemen. The men would pick them up and take them to a dance, or sometimes they would go to see them at their base but there had to be two men in the jeep, and one had to be armed so they didn't go to see them very often. Sometimes they would go to the makeshift movie where they sat on planks, which were hard as old boards. This was the only other activity aside from going to the O (officer's) club for dinner. One officer owned a boat and they would take the boat around the bay. Smitty and Tom soon were engaged to be married.

There was a little canteen where they could dance and this was where Jamie and Brad would meet and dance to the tunes of Frank Sinatra singing *Stardust, Sentimental Journey, Ole Buttermilk Sky* by the Kay Kyser orchestra, *Sunrise Serenade* by the Glenn Miller Orchestra, *You Belong To My Heart, There'll Be Bluebirds Over the White Cliffs of Dover,* and *We'll Meet Again* sung by Vera Lynn. They danced to their favorite song, *We'll Meet Again*, which would become their very own theme song.

Brad told Jamie about some of his combat missions. He started by telling her all about himself, where he grew up and how he became an aviator.

✰ ✰ ✰

Brad got interested in flying when he was a young boy in Rib Lake, Wisconsin. He would watch the old Curtis Jenny and the Bi-plane Waco 10 (which stood for Wichita Air Craft Company) fly right overhead and land on a grass field on his father's farm in all kinds of weather. Ben Toll, who was a good friend of the family, flew with Lindberg in the early mail/airline plane operation days and formed a company called Robertson Aircraft that eventually became American Airlines. Walt Steiner wound up flying for American Airlines at San Francisco, California, and Brad flew co-pilot with him. So, Brad really pretty much got in on the ground floor of the aviation world.

Brad went into the Army Air Corp in 1942.

Brad belonged to the 307th Bombardment Group, the 13th Army Air Corp. in the South and Southwest Pacific. More specifically, The Long Rangers.

Here in New Guinea Brad was participating in the ferocious fighting staged from the small air base in Nadzab. Nadzab is located in northeast New Guinea and fairly close to Finschhafen. Brad flew the B-24 Liberator made by Consolidated Vultee, which is a heavy bomber with four 1,200 horsepower engines. The plane had four turrets, a nose turret, tail, bottom and top and two hand held waist guns.

They didn't decorate their planes with beautiful women like a lot of other pilots did because they didn't fly the same plane each day. They flew what was serviceable.

His first combat mission was in 1944 in New Guinea. His flight was to Rabaul on New Britain and Wewak on a ground support mission on the north coast of New Guinea.

There were no fighter escorts unless the hops were short ones. If the fighters did accompany them, they flew with drop tanks. These were the P-38 twin-engine fighters. The B-24's were called the Long Rangers because they flew 11-hour flights. One of the longest flights was 16 hours to Java, Morotai to Palawan and to Saigon.

Very rarely did they fly in a complete formation. Most of the time their missions would take off at 10 o'clock in the evening, and then they would fly all night and be over their targets in daylight. "If you could rendezvous with 2, 3 or 4 planes that was great, but you didn't have the fuel to go around in circles to rendezvous. You would take what you had and go in."

His missions ran the gamut from support missions to bombing airports, and oil refining plants in Borneo. "We also did invasion support for landing forces in Borneo and skip bombing."

"When we did skip bombing, we pretended we were fighters. We would go in low over the water at 15 feet and pull up as we released the bomb and it skipped across the water and hit a ship. The bombardier was back in the bomb-bay before we started out on that, and he had to remove the nose fuses otherwise the bombs would go off underneath us when they hit the water. We only left the tail fuse in so it gave us time to get away. The B-24's were pretty cumbersome, and we'd get shot up pretty good sometimes."

Brad flew over the Moluccas, Noemfoor, Wewak, and Holandia on the coast of New Guinea. "We went to Biak which is the island just off the end of New Guinea and from there we went to the Moluccas to the northernmost island called Morotai."

"On Morotai, we only owned the airstrip. The Marine line was supposed to protect us but the Japanese came down the coast and swam around the guards and slit the pilots' throats while they slept. So the pilots then took turns guarding while the others slept.

"Washing Machine Charlie used to fly over every night just to harass us. He was flying in an open cockpit where he would throw his grenades over the side, like they did in World War I and make a general nuisance of himself. We sent up a lot of anti-aircraft fire and never hit him. It was a comedy. We couldn't get him, but sometimes we suffered from the shrapnel falling back down hitting a lot of our own people from our own guns. One night he did hit a plane. We were all lined up for a launch, and he hit one B-24 and all the planes up and down the taxiways went up on fire. It was a slaughter. We did eventually get him.

"At Mandai, we were hit badly. We were targeting the Borneo oil field. This was one of the missions that wasn't well thought out. Quite a few Zeros were working on our planes and we got shot up."

Brad was attacked by Six Zeros and Oscars as the overhead turret tore away quite a few of the control cables and left him with only a right elevator on the tail. It was uncontrolled flight going straight up and then they reached the apex, when they ran out of air speed and the nose dropped through forcing them straight down. At this point it took both pilots with their feet on the instrument panel and their arms around each control column yoke and both hands on each yoke, pulling aft, for the aircraft to recover to some semblance of level flight in a series of dives and climbs. The right gear was shot out and flaps shot out. "We could un-jam but needed to maintain constant pressure then we'd go too far and stall." When he got back from that mission the Commander was mad at him because Brad blew a tire on landing. Brad could have clobbered him!

"At the Balikpapan oilfields, there were 5 fighter fields in that vicinity. It was like hitting a hornet's nest. In this one mission, I couldn't form up with the 424th squadron. We were really fuel short and the rendezvous was haphazard and I never did form up with 424. The complete squadron was wiped out. I ended up forming up with another squadron from my group, out of the 4 squadrons we had. We couldn't stay in that formation for very long, so if you didn't get formed up on the first try you hooked up wherever you could. There were three different Jap planes, the Zekes, Oscars, and Zeros. The Oscars were the most prevalent, but were very similar to the Zeros. On this particular day, it was the Oscars that were after us. We were the second group to go in. The 424th, 370th, 372nd formed the group. So my screw-up saved my life I guess!"

It was not easy to have some time off to see Jamie, let alone being tired from his 11 to 14 hour flights, and then having to get a hop into Finschhafen to see her, but he was in love. Jamie was horrified by some of his flying stories but even more impressed with him for his flying skills and his incredible intelligence.

Brad flew a total of 36 missions with a total of 11 1/2 hours average flying time. He told Jamie, "Two of the missions I considered the worst were the Saigon mission and the mission to southern Celebes to Belkapapan. We were shot up pretty bad and didn't have fighter escort on either of them. We were, shot at by the fighter planes, and there were only two of us. They really worked us over, they shot out our controls and the plane was going straight up and down, it was a scary situation."

He was told when they were sent overseas if they were ever in a situation where they were going to be captured, to shoot the crew and commit suicide. "The torture the Japanese meted out was just beyond belief."

He would later say, "My life on that dairy farm where I grew up was ground training for the Army Air Corps."

After awhile Jamie was very busy and Brad was also very busy flying missions, and so they didn't see each other very often. A romance was difficult at best in the wartime situation.

✡ ✡ ✡

Jamie had only been in New Guinea several months. It was a Rope-yarn Sunday, which means a stand-down day, so people were quiet. They had been working hard all week to finish the hospital. The hospital was half finished when the nurses arrived in New Guinea and the Seabees and the nurses and all available hands helped to try to finish the hospital. The nurses were relaxing from a hard week at work, sitting on the concrete porch in front of their quarters. A languid breeze rustled the palm fronds and the clean smelling laundry on the line, Jamie had just washed her hair and was sitting in the sun to let it dry when an Army sergeant came running into the camp screaming, "We can't find the captain. We have searched the whole base and we can't find her." Jamie had had a creepy feeling about the nurse. She had been depressed for several weeks. Jamie being the take charge person that she was, said, "Have you done a square search?" "No Ma'am, but I will start it right away." The yeoman understood and right away got a group together to start a square search. After a search of the base was made, a search team was launched and men fanned out into the jungle. After about twenty minutes of searching, they found that beautiful young captain lying in the jungle underbrush. It was a horrible sight. She had gone out into the jungle and had taken Phenobarbital and wrapped jungle vine greenery around her neck. She wanted to make sure she died. Jamie said, "I guess the war was too much of a shock for our chief nurse."

Jamie remembered back to what she had said only several weeks before, "The captain couldn't get over the strained looks of our men." She realized this was maybe why the captain had committed suicide. That was quite a shock to the nurses - all of a sudden the war and being a nurse in this strange place was no longer an adventure. It was serious business with devastating consequences. She was a captain and they all, being new nurses, had looked up to her for guidance. Here they were, stranded on this island, feeling now rather insecure. As if this weren't enough of a shock, the colonel of the base called everyone together and proceeded to say they were all to blame for the captain's death. How unfair for him to shift the blame to all of them. They were traumatized by her death. She was a war casualty, one who simply couldn't stand the pressure. It had all been so unreal. It brought the war up front and center.

Instead of being suffocated by the enormity of this tragedy, Jamie committed herself to being there for the other nurses as a strong and caring superior officer who would help her nurses now and in the future. She told herself there is always something good that comes out of something bad, and she soldiered on. She would remember that for all of her life. This incident had profoundly impacted Jamie's thinking and would be evident when she volunteered later to go to Vietnam. Everyone on the base mourned the captain's passing.

✡ ✡ ✡

Although the seizure of Port Moresby might have to be postponed, Japan had no intention of abandoning that goal or any other objective necessary to achieve victory. Admiral Yamamoto had a plan he was certain would lure the enemy's aircraft carriers to their doom and end American hopes of winning the war in the Pacific.

The enemy was now encroaching and it was no longer safe for the nurses to be located in New Guinea, so they were going to be transferred to the Philippines.

Jamie met a priest, Father Quinan, who was a patient. She said to the priest, "You know, I have always gone to Catholic mass with my friends when I was in Chicago but there was this little Catholic Church in my home town and I thought I'd always like to be a Catholic."

He said, "Well, I'll give instructions," and he baptized her and confirmed her into the Catholic faith.

Two days before Jamie left New Guinea she and the nurses went to a very primitive native village to have a luau with the local natives who used to be cannibals. Brad had set up the meeting of American nurses and the New Guineans. He took them up in the hills in a jeep. She wasn't afraid to go to this village. She remarked to a friend, "I wasn't afraid of anything in my life, I probably should have been, but I wasn't." The Army had hired the natives to be their guards at the hospitals. They dressed them like policemen but they wore shorts because it was so hot. These same people looked ferocious in their native garb, and the faint of heart would have been frightened, but not Jamie.

It was Jamie's next to the last day in New Guinea. She had just been informed she and the other nurses had orders to leave New Guinea because the enemy was coming closer and they needed to be moved to a forward position in the Philippines. It was short notice and Jamie was very upset because her romance with Brad was being cut short.

Jamie was very thankful she could get in touch with Brad and they could meet at the luau. Sometimes it was difficult to make contact. Brad had just come back from one of his horrendous flights and survived again. Jamie thought it was truly amazing what that man would go through each day, and she so admired him for his patriotism and skill in flying. Brad had proposed to her several times but Jamie, with agonized heart, would have to tell Brad she had to go to her new duty station in the Philippines the next day. It was no longer safe for the nurses to be in New Guinea. The departure date had come up very fast, and her head was swimming. Brad was the love of her life and she could not bear to think of life without him. She had fallen so deeply in love with him. He was so kind and so romantic and so in love with her.

It was early evening with a soft wind blowing and Jamie was waiting patiently in a little flower garden with a wooden bench. When she saw him her heart skipped a beat as it always had, and when he saw her, that wonderful smile spread across his handsome face.

He gently took her hand in his hand and kissed it, and kissed her softly on the cheek as he sat down on the wooden bench next to Jamie. He kissed her again and told her of his love for her. When they kissed and he held her in his arms, the war seemed oddly far away and all sound or anything else in the world disappeared. It was just Brad and herself holding each other in their love. It brought tears to her eyes. He spoke of his flying missions and how he kept thinking about her and how he had to get back to her because she was all he lived for now. He wanted her safely back home in the states where he knew she would be safe and she would belong to him. They had talked about the possibility of their future together, of having children and settling down. He told her of his love for her and when he spoke to her she knew he was the right man. But a war was waging inside of her. She had agonized over whether she should give in to her selfish longings and marry Brad or continue with her career. It was a bittersweet love and she was being torn apart because of her indecision. It was like two romances. She had a romance with Brad, and a romance with the Army. Brad had asked her several times to marry him. She had made her decision for now. The way was clear to her. She was dedicated to being an Army nurse. Partly her decision was the commitment she made when she joined the Army, to complete the mission. She owed her allegiance to her country and the men who were fighting to protect it.

Brad was devastated. She couldn't bear to hurt him. She couldn't believe the pain she had caused him. But while she agonized over the pain she had just inflicted on him in turning down his proposal of marriage, she had to be true to herself. While she loved him dearly, and probably always would, she had really come to terms with her life. She felt she was going in the face of uncertain consequences, in war, not knowing what would be at the next turn of events in her life. But she had a heightened awareness of who she was now and where she was going. At great personal sacrifice of giving up a life with her true love, she decided she could not have a life with him. At this point in time she was going to devote her life to her duty to her patients, and thus serve a greater purpose than her own personal life. She had an enormous storehouse of love to give to her patients, which regenerated daily. One of the deciding factors was the suicide of the captain, and how shocked her fellow nurses were at this suicide, and she wanted to be there for them and future nurses in their hour of need. She wanted to be that stalwart leader they could depend on. This was the beauty of Jamie. She had been shaped and molded for her future as a career nurse here in New Guinea. She had finally resolved she had set her course of being a nurse and as much as she loved Brad, she would not be deterred. She was resilient and strong, and she had a great mission in life of aiding the wounded men in the war and serving her country. It had been like a relationship with two men, between her desire to marry Brad, and her desire to continue with her career. Then she realized her career was the right man for her.

But, devastated as he was, Brad promised to write to her in the hope she would either change her mind or be stationed with him at a new destination. He thought it might be hopeless because he knew now just how dedicated she was to her nursing career but he would hold onto hope and try to keep track of her. This was all he could do now. It was a tearful parting with the knowledge they might never see each other ever again. At the end of their conversation, Jamie touched his face and kissed his cheek and simply said, "Goodbye for now."

After Jamie left to be stationed in the Philippines, General Douglas MacArthur's forces in the South Pacific were advancing westward through New Guinea. In a series of amphibious operations along the coast and against offshore islands, covered by airpower, he worked his way up the northern coast of the island and by August 1944 he was in control of all New Guinea. Japan had been relying on oil to lubricate its war machine from the Celebes, Borneo and eastern Java. With supplies cut off, it was only a matter of time. Macarthur's next objective would be the Philippines and, in the fall, the attack carriers would join him there. On October 25, 1944 General MacArthur would fulfill his promise and would return to the Philippines.

CHAPTER 9

The Philippines at War's End

In 1945, Jamie was sent to Manila in the Philippines. It was hot and muggy, and there was a stench in the air. There were big craters in the ground, all the trees had been defoliated and buildings were bombed out. The mass of humanity in this section of Manila had been freed and were milling about scrounging for food.

Jamie was headquartered in the Santo Tomas hospital that had been a POW camp. The Japanese had been driven out of this small sector of Manila, leaving the prisoners behind. A lot of wounded were sent to Jamie after being liberated. They had been hungry for so long they would go to the food cart and eat right out of the bowls with huge soupspoons. They forgot all discipline. One of the hardest things she ever had to do was to deny food to the POWs. If she had let them eat all they wanted they would have become very ill, and possibly died.

The men were crammed into several rooms, head to toe, and lined up in row upon row of cots. They were disease ridden and emaciated. Army food soon arrived consisting of potatoes, gravy, spam, and vegetables. Quite a change from the small daily portion of rice they had received from the Japanese.

She was serving as Head Nurse at this busy duty station. She had to get most of the POWs out of there quickly and back to the States. But she had to make sure they had gained some weight first.

When the nurses went about in a vehicle there had to be two men in uniform accompanying them and one of them had to be armed, because the enemy was still close by.

Her brother Robert, who was Petty Officer First Class in the Navy, had been trying to get to her during the entire war, with no success, but when she was sent to Manila, he was also ordered to Subic Bay. He came in to see her on a supply truck, risking his life going through enemy territory. They talked for two hours and finally she said, "You'd better get back to base."

"Yes, I'd better because I won't have any place to sleep tonight if I don't." Soon after he left she could hear artillery fire throughout the jungle and her heart sank. She thought, "Oh my God, are the Japanese trying to retake the city?" At first she thought her brother was in danger, but it wasn't he they were shooting at. Everyone had just heard the war was over, and they were shooting everything they could find into the air. What rejoicing! The war was finally over. His coming to see her was very memorable for her.

Jamie returned to her patients who were the former American POW's. They were all so emaciated. Her special patient was John Boswell. This once handsome light brown haired, blue-eyed man who weighed 220 pounds when he joined the Marines, was now 110 pounds. He had just been transferred in from Japan. He seemed to have gone through the most in the POW camps. Though being emaciated and scarred, he was alive, and he had such a tremendous spirit. She guessed this was what had carried him through his worst moments in captivity. His memories were permanently etched in his mind. Jamie encouraged him to tell her his story.

He spoke slowly at first, and as the story began to unfold, he spoke quickly, the words spilling out. "Corregidor was divided into three sections. Bottom side, (lower level), Middle side and Topside, the hilly part of Corregidor. We got billeted at Middle side. They told us Middle side barracks was bomb proof and were convinced the Japs would not bomb Corregidor. They urged us to relax and enjoy ourselves.

"December 29, 1941 is a day I will never forget. The air raid siren began to sound off. The Army guys continued to play pool. Marines were ordered to go immediately to the ground floor. Col. Murphy was in charge of our quarters. While he was checking to see all Marines had cleared the area, bombs began to hit the barracks. Murphy was killed by one of the first bombs. The bombs penetrated every deck and exploded on the ground floor. So much for being bomb proof.

"On Corregidor, I set my machine gun section positions and continued to improve our defense against air and ground bombardment. Aerial bombardments during the day became routine. Later, harassing night runs were added to the daylight runs. The night runs were done by a small plane, as its motor sounded like a washing machine, the night runs became known as Washing Machine Charlie. Evidently, the purpose of these night runs was to disturb our rest or sleep.

"As the battle for Bataan unfolded, it became clear there were no reserve troops to give front line troops a rest. Food, ammo and medicine were in very short supply.

"Bataan surrendered on April 9, 1942. I could actually observe with my binoculars as I sat in my foxhole, the beginning of what was to become known as the Bataan Death March. Little did I realize the honorable soldiers of the emperor were about to violate the fundamental laws of human decency. More than 10,000 American and Philippine prisoners on the march were flattened by tank treads, shot, bayoneted, beaten to death with rifles, denied food and water and pushed beyond human endurance until many died from complete and total exhaustion.

"Two days after Bataan surrendered General MacArthur left Corregidor for Mindanao by PT boat and continued by plane to Australia, taking his family and all household belongings with him. Before leaving he issued a bulletin to the troops, which said: 'Help is on the way. Hundreds of ships with food and thousands of men are on the way.' These proved to be idle words. MacArthur became one of the most hated among the men on Bataan and Corregidor.

"As the bombardments intensified on Corregidor, those of us on beach defense intended to stay near our guns day and night. Our main activity was digging deeper and better foxholes and tunnels to protect ourselves and our weapons. Any movement on Corregidor by the Japs usually resulted in a barrage of artillery fire from Bataan.

"General Wainwright, who was put in charge after MacArthur left, realized the hopelessness of the situation. Though he was supposed to fight to the bitter end, he did not want any more unnecessary bloodshed and surrendered the entire regiment when the Japs invaded Corregidor. The invasion troops were many thousands strong and had the latest in equipment to fight with. The American forces would have had no chance to win and would most likely have been annihilated to the last man. Wainwright was later reprimanded for doing so but it was the only humane thing to do at the time. The surrender came on May 5th, my 22nd birthday!

"On May 6, 1942, we officially became prisoners of the Japanese. We had no idea what was in store for us, we could only hope for the best.

"Few of us had ever heard of the Bushido code, the fighting code of the Japanese warrior. According to this code surrender was considered cowardice. Death was the alternative. A person who surrendered in the eyes of the Imperial Forces of Japan was humanity in its lowest form. Any show of pity, sympathy or compassion was unmanly and violated the Bushido code. Barbaric behavior, such as, murder, rape, pillage and torture was acceptable.

"On May 24 we were put aboard a ship and brought to Manila. The boats with prisoners were anchored off shore and we were forced to swim or wade ashore. Waiting on the shore were Japanese officers on horseback who formed us into a column and paraded us through the streets of Manila, down Dewey Blvd, to the old Philippine Prison of Bilibid. Bilibid was to become a repair shop for prisoners serving at slave labor camps throughout the Philippines who became victims of beatings, disease or accidents. They had a couple of doctors, and some very primitive hospital facilities. My friend Bob Martineau, who could not do much work with only one leg, spent his entire prison time in Bilibid.

"We used open pit urinals and privies with flies everywhere. Meaningful medical treatment was not available. Repeated pleas to the Japs for medicine and food were ignored. One of the bamboo shacks was designated as a hospital. When a prisoner reached a point where he could no longer take care of basic functions he was moved to the hospital shack as a patient and given whatever medical treatment was possible, administered with sympathy and encouragement by the American medical personnel, who were also subjected to the same conditions as the other prisoners. The only real medication available was aspirin. For dysentery, the sick were given burnt rice.

"When a patient's condition deteriorated to the point that death was imminent, he was moved to the zero ward, meaning there was zero chance for survival. I was assigned to remove the dead from the zero-ward and bury them.

"Our only food consisted of Lugao, a watery rice mixture. Soon a song made the rounds.

> Lugao, Lugao,
> Eat the stuff, you must.
> If you eat till satisfied
> Belly belly bust.
> You no eat then you die
> Isn't nature grand?
> MacArthur come and liberate
> the bastards of Bataan.

"Many prisoners thought about escape and several tried it. This brought great difficulties because you did not know whom to contact after you escaped. Often escapees were returned for prize money and immediately shot by the Japs, who soon came up with a solution to the escape problem. The prisoners were divided into groups of ten. If one of the ten would escape, the other nine would be shot or decapitated.

"Many wonderful Filipino people risked their lives time and time again to get food to prisoners, while others carried secret messages to and from internment camps for family members of the prisoners. If caught it meant brutal punishment, then execution, usually by beheading.

"It was while at Cabanatuan that I made a serious assessment of my situation and gave much thought to what I could do to increase my chance of survival. I accepted the fact I was now at the mercy of barbarians who considered compassion unmanly and a sign of weakness. The starvation diet of a little rice and whistle weed soup would not sustain a person long. The lack of sanitary conditions could only result in more flies, more disease and more deaths. So I made my plans carefully. First, I would keep a low profile, blending in with the crowd, thus reducing my chance of random beatings or execution. Then, I would get the hell out of there if the opportunity ever presented itself. In the meantime I made a resolution to find at least one thing each day to laugh or smile about. I also wanted to find something of beauty, something I could admire.

"In August I noticed a work detail being formed of about four hundred men. I had no idea where it was going but I quietly joined the group. Unfortunately the detail was headed for Palawan Island.

"I was in the Palawan slave labor camp from September until mid December 1942. We prisoners were to clear a jungle using picks, axes, shovels and shoulder poles with sacks suspended from them for carrying dirt from place to place to fill or build up another area. Our task was to transform a jungle into an airfield landing strip. The taskmasters were brutal, the work difficult and demanding, the weather extremely hot and humid and the rice wormy and in short supply.

"As for clothing, the Japs never issued us new clothes. With the intense heat and humidity, in addition to the monsoons, our original clothes had simply rotted away. We had nothing left. I worked in a G-string with no protection from the relentless sun. I often wished I had a hat.

"We did have some laughs, though, which helped our morale. There was a very short pudgy Jap officer whose daily early morning routine was to show his skills with his samurai sword. We were supposed to watch this, after first bowing to the Emperor. He wore tall boots and we gave him the nickname: Puss N' Boots. He would shout and gyrate, lift the sword high above his head, swinging it backward until it almost hit the ground. One time, as he was swinging the sword backward it hit him right in the fanny. We all cheered and applauded. He never went through this routine again.

"We did try to sabotage the work. To cut the trees down in the jungle we had to work in pairs with a cross cut saw. This work to me was a breeze; I had done this at home many times. But we all acted as if it was very difficult and slowed it down. Also, we often removed the stakes the Japs had set out to outline the airfield.

"Once while thinking how hungry I was, I noticed a papaya tree near the compound fence with ripe fruit hanging above the fence. Not seeing any guards close by I took a chance and picked a papaya. Alas, Sergeant Nitchitoni caught me. This Jap was a brutal, sadistic guard, who enjoyed inflicting pain and suffering on American prisoners. He would hit prisoners with whatever weapon he could grab and also supervised subordinates who flogged prisoners, while the prisoners arms were tied around trees and lashed so tight they could not fall down. Nichitoni would stand by, holding a pistol to the prisoner's head. When he caught me with the papaya he took a piece of steel used to re-enforce cement and started beating me with it. He beat me from my head to my feet for an extended period of time, resulting in broken bones in my arm, neck and back. Apparently my kidneys were damaged as well, as I urinated blood for many weeks.

"The American doctor made a makeshift splint for my broken arms out of chicken wire, apologizing that that was the best he could do. A few days later I was sent to Bilibid prison for repairs. Little did I know at that time this severe beating saved my life, I never was sent back to Palawan. The men who stayed there were massacred by the Japs in December 1944, about one hundred fifty in all. A few escaped to tell the world about it.

"Overall conditions in Bilibid were better than in any other of the prison camps. I wished I could have stayed longer. When I was declared healthy enough to go back to work I was transported to Cabanatuan Camp I.

"My job was not that bad in this camp. I had to work on the farm which meant I had an opportunity once in awhile to steal some fresh vegetables. I had to carry a five-gallon bucket with water from a creek up and down a hill to the farm.

"At night we slept in barracks on bamboo slats. Inside, the lice and bed bugs ate you up. Outside the mosquitoes and ants would take their turn.

"The worst were the flies. They were all around and caused a lot of diseases. Colonel Beecher, our Senior POW officer organized a fly abatement program and managed to convince the Japs to allow POWs to collect flies and gave them a few cigarettes in exchange.

"On September 21, 1944, while working on an airfield, the Japs wanted the prisoners to build at the prison camp of Las Pinas near Manila, an old Navy Chief in our group yelled out to me: 'Boswell, I hear planes and they are not Jap planes.' My response was: 'Wishful thinking, Chief.' But he was right. Soon after, Jap planes were falling in flames all around. American planes began to strafe our area as we were yelling and screaming to see the Japs being clobbered. Two Navy planes started strafing where we were, wagging their wings as they passed. American planes shot down every Jap in sight and bombs were falling in the Manila port area.

"On October 1, 1944, we were moved to Manila, then loaded aboard the Hell Ship Haro Maru, for a journey into hell that defies description.

"Jap officers with swords drawn and enlisted Japs with rifles with fixed bayonets pushed and shoved POWs against the rear wall, shoulder to shoulder and back against the wall. The second row backs against chests of the first row. Loading continued in this manner until the hold was jammed with 700 POWs. Standing room only. About 400 POWs were packed in a smaller aft hold. Neither had toilets or water. When the loading of prisoners had been completed, the Japs secured all escape routes, leaving a small area, enough for two people, to exit the hold at the same time. Four prisoners were assigned to this opening. It did not take long before suffocation, dehydration and heat exhaustion began to take its toll. Lack of fresh air caused many deaths. On October 3, 1944, the Haro Maru, which we called the Horror Maru or Benjo Maru (benjo is Japanese for toilet), got under way, joining a convoy of merchant ships, tankers and escorting naval vessels. Many of these ships were sunk by American subs or aircraft. None of the Jap ships had any markings that POWs were aboard.

"Four POWs were assigned to the Bucket detail. Each had a five-gallon bucket. They lowered empty buckets into the hold for human waste and pulled them up when filled. They were then dumped over the side. Each morning bodies of POWs who had died during the night were tied to ropes, pulled up on deck and dumped over the sides."

At this point, John stopped talking and was struggling to keep his composure. He said, "I'm not sure I can continue."

Jamie touched his shoulder lightly and said, "This is good therapy. You need to talk."

He said, "This was one of the hardest parts of being in captivity on the Hell Ship.

Once a day another bucket was lowered with rice balls, our only food each day. We also were told to send our canteens up, hopefully to be filled with water. The canteen became a weapon of life and death. It was life if your canteen happened to be one that got filled and returned to you. Some prisoners went delirious from lack of water, some even tried to kill their fellow men for a sip. One day, my canteen did not come back. I was almost totally dehydrated and would not have lasted through the night if not for my buddy Charlie Kirklen, who shared his water with me, not knowing if he would get another ration himself. I took a replacement canteen cup from a prisoner who had died during the night.

"Miraculously our ship was spared, apparently the only ship in the convoy. Later I heard only three ships in our entire convoy had made it.

"Arriving in Moji, Japan on January 23, 1945, the POWs were put ashore January 25 in subfreezing weather, wearing what little was left of our tropical clothing and, if lucky, discarded Jap uniforms. On January 28 we arrived at Sendai Sub-Camp 3B near the Hosokura lead and zinc mine, which was part of the Mitsubishi Mining Co. We were led on foot along a small trail of packed snow to an old unheated wooden building, which we soon named the ice box. This became our home for the remainder of the war.

"A new routine became established for prisoners. Early in the morning, after a miserably cold night in the Ice Box, we ate a little breakfast consisting of barley mixed with a bit of rice. Then we were marched to the mine.

"The cold took its toll. Men began to die from cold and exposure. Pneumonia was the big killer. Also a lot of prisoners got beriberi. The ground was frozen so hard it was not possible to dig graves for those who died, so the bodies were stacked in a small shed until the spring thaw.

"I came down with pneumonia in February, and two weeks of my life became a complete blank. The last thing I remember before I blacked out was severe chest-pains with each breath I took. When I woke up I found myself in a small isolated room with other sick prisoners. Two American Army doctors were in charge. One told me how lucky I was the Japs had decided to release some Red Cross medical supplies. He then told me that I had been unconscious for two weeks and that they had not expected me to live.

"Just a few days after I came out of the coma, our Colonel informed me that the Japs insisted that I go back to work.

"We tried our best to sabotage the work in the mines. For instance, each time they blasted, we quickly blew out our lamps, pretending the blast caused it. This delayed the procedures. Other times we were able to put rocks on the rail of the mine carts, making them flip over. Day after miserable day slowly passed as we struggled to survive.

"Spring finally arrived in Hosokura. We began to thaw out and life was a little less miserable. At the end of March all of us received a large Red Cross package with food and clothing, a very welcome gift indeed!

"One day in August a Swiss Red Cross representative came into the camp and told us about the dropping of the atom bombs. The work in the mines suddenly ceased, Jap guards were gone. They had left so suddenly that they left their rifles behind. Only a Jap commandant was left who started shouting at us: 'You have to gain weight, you have to gain weight.' He probably was worried he would be punished when the rescuers found us in such a deplorable condition.

"The order to move out finally reached us and we were taken by train to Sendai for delousing, processing and rehabilitation.

"When I was checked by the medical team at Sendai my request to fly home was disapproved because of my condition. I was barely able to walk. I had a lot of open sores and my weight, once 220 lbs, had dropped to 110 lbs. I became a bed patient in the Philippines. Thank God I had survived! It would be discovered later that 37 percent of the men captured by the Japs had not been that lucky."

Jamie was honored to have John as her patient. She was so touched by John's sacrifice, and that of the other men. She realized sacrifice builds strength, and his strength had built hope for him. The stress of being caught in a situation with no way out must have been overwhelming to most of the men. A lot of the men didn't survive, but John always had hope.

Was there any sanity in a world gone mad? He had wondered desperately about this for four long years, and he found the sanity, love, and kindness in someone who cared about his well being, and this is why he wanted to tell Jamie his story.

John was soon in fairly good shape, after all of Jamie's good care, and sent home for six more months to recuperate in the Veterans' Administration hospital in Florida, which was close to his home.

Jamie was pleased she had nursed so many POWs back to fairly good health.

August 15th was the long awaited day, VJ day = Victory over Japan. People had changed during the war. The women at home had become very independent. Life was forever changed in the world. People in

Japan heard the Emperor's voice for the first time in history. The bombs had been dropped on Hiroshima and Nagasaki forcing the Japanese to surrender. On September 2nd General MacArthur spoke of a better world at the ceremony on the battleship Missouri in Tokyo Bay, as Japan and the allies signed the documents ending the war. As MacArthur said, "It is for us, both victors and vanquished, to rise to that higher dignity which alone benefits the sacred purposes we are about to serve.

In April of that year Roosevelt had died short of the eve of victory, and Harry S. Truman assumed the presidency.

On May 7th the war had ended in Europe.

On July 16, 1945, Jamie, still in Manila in the Philippines went swimming in a pool on the base. Rowdy aviators pushed her into the pool and she tore her similar cartilage in her right knee, so she couldn't bear weight on that leg. They took her to surgery but couldn't reduce the close reduction on it. They sent her stateside.

She was flown into Travis Air Force Base in California. Jamie returned to the US on September 12, 1945. Her whole family came to greet her, all sorts of Jamison's were there! What a reunion! She was at Travis for several days, and then flown to Illinois where she would be close to home. At this point she didn't know if she would ever be able to walk again or be on crutches for all of her life.

Then they sent her to Mayo General Hospital at Galesburg, Illinois as a patient on 19 September 1945 and she finally got to where she could walk on her leg.

CHAPTER 10

Ft. Sam Houston, Texas

Jamie was sent to Ft. Sam Houston, Texas and worked there as 1st Lieutenant for 36 months. She was Charge Nurse of the ward and then supervisor of the Neuropsychiatric section later. She instructed nurses and corpsmen in special duties and procedures on these wards. She gave intravenous sedations, and sedative packs and tubs and supervised their personal hygiene care. She also administered sulfa drugs and penicillin. She treated skin diseases and dehydration and emaciated cases of those released from POW camps in Asia.

A lot of people were getting out of the service. The war was over and they didn't see any point in staying in. Her two brothers got out of the service at this time also. They were going to get on with their lives. She decided she wanted to get out of the service too. She was discharged from the Army at BAMC Thirteenth General hospital, APO 75, on May 11, 1946 at Ft. Sam Houston, Texas. She always wondered whether Brad had survived.

✬ ✬ ✬

Jamie was on inactive status from the Army from 12 May 1946 to 15 August 1948 and working at Winters Veterans Administration hospital in Topeka, Kansas, serving as Neuropsychiatric Nurse. She had treated the POWs and the injured from the war but they were older men and Jamie decided she wanted to be a nurse to the younger men. She enjoyed talking to them more than the older men. The Army hadn't really discharged her, they had only discharged her from active duty, and they kept her on inactive duty status so they could call her back. She decided to go back to active duty.

She was happy to be back in Kansas because she was able to be with her sister-in-law Mavis when she had her first two children. Her brother

Bert had been a Seaman 1st Class on a Tanker. He made it to the end of the war. Her older brother Robert was in the hospital for a hernia operation and met a young woman who had joined the Waves.

Her brother Bert and Mavis's brother had their hernias repaired and they were in beds right next to each other. Mavis went to visit her brother and that's how she met Jamie's brother. They got married and moved back to Iowa.

At the end of the war, the stores were depleted after four years of struggle and Jamie's mother asked Jamie, "What will I give Bert and Mavis for a wedding present?"

Jamie replied, "Give them the tablecloth you made for me during the war."

Jamie was present when her first niece was born, and was there to assist Mavis during the delivery. Ann was Bert and Mavis' first child. Jamie administered gas so Mavis wasn't so uncomfortable. Jamie was the first one to hold the baby.

In 1949 Robert, Jamie's oldest brother, 10 years older than Jamie and 39 years old at this time, met his future wife at a VFW post in St. Louis, Missouri. They had only known each other for 2 months and were married in August 1949 in Kansas City. Ester and Susie were born in Kansas City. Robert opened a store there. Ester was born January of 1953 and Jamie was present when she was born. Susie was born in October 1954.

Bert's other two children David and Pam, were born later, but Jamie was at another duty station by then.

Bert became a teacher and set up a credit union in Concordia, Kansas where he was teaching. People needed financial help and this was the only way they could do it. He also was running a store and she went to help him. Jamie and her Father bought the store and her Father ran it while Jamie was in Japan later on.

While she was working for the Veterans Administration in Topeka, Kansas, her old boyfriend, Brad, from New Guinea paid her a surprise visit. They spent a lot of time together. Brad and Jamie went to their old friends from New Guinea, Smitty and Mac's wedding, which was in Rockford Illinois.

Brad was in Washington at this time and they went dancing when he could get away from work. He was still not married. He had devotedly been writing to her at each of her duty stations. They had a serious talk and he told her he couldn't get her out of his mind and she knew he still loved her, but they didn't make any future plans at this time.

It was 1946 and the Big Bands were popular. People danced to hit tunes like *As Time Goes By* by Dooley Wilson, *Boogie Woogie Bugle Boy of Company B* by the Andrew sisters, *Coming In On A Wing And A Prayer* sung by the Song Spinners, *G.I. Jive* by Johnny Mercer, *I Left My Heart At The Stage Door Canteen* by the Sammy Kaye Orchestra, *I'll Get By As Long As I Have You* by Harry James Orchestra, *Is You Is Or Is You Ain't My Baby* by Louis Jordan Orchestra, *Ole Buttermilk Sky* by Kay Kyser Orchestra, *Sentimental Journey* by Les Brown Orchestra, and *Stardust* by Frank Sinatra and the Pied Pipers.

CHAPTER 11

Back in the Army

Jamie was back in the Army. As her first assignment, she was appointed to the rank of First Lieutenant, Army Nurse Corps on April 28, 1948, and she was sent to Walter Reed AMC in Washington, D.C. where she served from September 1, 1948 until February 28, 1950.

Jamie was appointed the rank of Captain on July 27, 1949. She was a General Duty nurse on both officers' and women's closed psychiatric wards, assisting the physician in administration of therapeutic measures and drugs in the treatment of mentally ill patients and observed and recorded patients behavior. She also supervised subsidiary workers in detailed assignments. She managed patients and personnel in her kind but firm way. With her outgoing personality, she made many friends at this duty station and enjoyed a lot of social activities there. She enjoyed knitting, sewing and photography.

March 1 to July 1950 Jamie served at Walter Reed hospital as psychiatric nurse on the women's wards for both disturbed and quiet psychiatric patients. She had many long tension-filled sessions assisting doctors with treatments including electro-shock therapy. These sessions were difficult for Jamie.

✿ ✿ ✿

On September 1, 1950 Jamie was sent to U.S. Naval Hospital at Portsmouth, Virginia. As a General Duty nurse she had a tour with the Navy. They were experimenting back and forth and they would have them work in the Army and then the Navy.

Jamie seemed to be adapting well to Navy routine. She was supervisor of a medical ward and responsible for the nursing care of patients, dispensing medications and giving treatments and teaching and supervising duties of the hospital corpsmen, maintenance of the ward and its equipment, housekeeping and sanitation and maintenance of all records, charts and reports and ward discipline. She met all emergencies well.

The hospital was so old it had walls three feet thick. They meant for it to last forever and they are still probably using it. It wouldn't fall down, even if it were shelled. This is probably why they built it that way. She served there a short time and then the Navy decided to dispense with the trial period and sent her back to the Army. She didn't know why, because she got along with the Navy and she thought everybody else did, too.

Jamie made a lot of friends at Portsmouth in the short time she was there. She had missed the sense of family of being a nurse in the Army. No civilian can ever understand the feelings you have. She served there until October 31, 1950.

✢ ✢ ✢

Jamie's next tour of duty was Ft. Monroe, in Hampton, Virginia, where she served for six months. They took her there by helicopter, November 1, 1950.

Ft. Monroe was small with 500 officers and 500 enlisted men. It was an old building built during the civil war. General Lee used to live on the grounds. This hospital was one of Jamie's favorites.

At Ft. Monroe her duties were general duty on Medical, Surgical, Obstetrical Wards and the Nursery. She was Head Nurse in planning schedules and care of all types of patients. She was a good listener, and was well liked by the patients. She enjoyed assisting in the delivery room and nursery. She gave pre-and post-partum care and supervised non-professional personnel. She was a Clinic Nurse responsible for all immunizations and records and assisted the doctors. She was maturing and working very well under pressure and she had a lot of common sense. She was the sort of person others went to for advice. She was economical in the use of supplies. She was sometimes inclined to be over-confident.

July 31, 1950 President Truman authorized a military buildup to fight in Korea against Chinese Communist aggression. General MacArthur was appointed Chief of the U.N. Forces.

While Jamie was stationed at Ft. Monroe, she took a weekend pass and went to Virginia Beach with a couple of friends and all of a sudden they heard sound trucks broadcasting, "Will all military personnel return to their base." They got in the car and drove back to Washington. War had just broken out against North Korea.

The Army gave 24 hours notice to pack up and be ready to move for those people being sent to Korea.

On April 20, 1951, MacArthur, one of our country's most heroic generals, gave his farewell speech in Congress. He borrowed a line from an old barrack ballad of the day. "Old soldiers never die, they just fade away, and now I close my military career and just fade away." Everyone at Ft. Monroe was sitting in the cafeteria watching it on TV. Jamie was so affected by his speech, especially since she had seen him in Australia, and knew of his history as an Army general. There was not a dry eye in the place. It was so sad for everyone to see him, as he said, just fade away.

Just six months later, on November 28, 1951, a truce line was established at the 38th parallel in Korea, creating a neutral zone, but the war would go on between the North and the South for another two years. The shooting would stop on July 28, 1953, and a peace treaty would be signed at Panmunjom.

Children would come in to visit with Jamie. Three of them were always on the steps to her house. They were there after her shift in the afternoon and all they wanted to do was play. They would go in and put on some of her clothes and entertain her. Her mother came out to ask her to come in and help her pack and these kids kept coming in and taking the clothes out of the suitcase, she packed them again and the first thing she knew they had them out again. Jamie was packing for her next duty station, which was to be in Japan.

CHAPTER 12

Japan

Jamie's new orders with the rank of Captain now were to Yokohama Japan. She arrived there December 17, 1952. Yokohama is just north of Tokyo. It was there Commodore Perry landed in his Black Ships in 1853. By the time Jamie got to Japan it had been resurrected from the 2nd World War by General MacArthur from 1945 to 1949. At this time he was a five star general which is the highest rank achievable in any branch of the military. He was Supreme Commander of the Allied Powers.

In 1947 under the new constitution, the emperor lost all political and military power and was made a symbol of the state. Japan was forbidden to ever wage a war or to have an Army again. MacArthur imposed rigid censorship of any anti-American topics, and because of this ruling, cooperation worked smoothly between the Japanese and the allied powers.

In Japanese mythology, the Sun Goddess Amaterasu ruled in 660 B.C. It is believed the emperor ruled over Japan for 1500 years and all rulers were descended from the first divine Imperial family. Shinto gods are called Kami which are sacred spirits. Humans become Kami when they die and are revered by their family. Kami of extraordinary people are worshipped at some of the shrines. The Sun Goddess is Shinto's most important Kami. Followers of Shinto believe all humans are good, and evil is caused by evil spirits. Rituals are performed by the Shinto priests to keep away the evil spirits. Kami are also sacred spirits such as rain and wind, and these spirits live in trees, rivers, rocks and mountains. This is why Japanese have such beautiful gardens.

When MacArthur wrote the new constitution deposing the emperor, he knew the nation would be drastically changed. He also broke up the concentration of power in large companies and decentralized the school systems and police departments. The Korean War helped to accelerate Japan's economy and living standards. The new Liberal Democratic Party MacArthur had created had a strong stabilizing effect. Having lost the 2nd World War, the Japanese were very receptive to new ideas - provided their emperor Hirohito was not prosecuted for war crimes. He was not prosecuted and remained as a figurehead. MacArthur wanted a free market economy based on medium sized companies and he also wanted Japan to be a welfare state. Many powerful Wall Street moguls in the United States objected to this because they wanted to see a stronger ally as a democracy in the Orient. In 1948 the U.S. government ordered MacArthur to revive heavy industry in Japan and increase exports while reducing government spending and social welfare. They didn't realize at the time they had unwittingly unleashed an economic giant that would eventually compete with the United States. MacArthur was not in Japan long when he was called to command forces that were going to invade North Korea.

MacArthur planned an attack on Inch on, Korea and he managed to push the North Koreans to the Communist China border, but the Chinese Communists pushed his forces back. MacArthur asked President Truman if the war could be expanded to a war with China but his request was denied and General MacArthur was subsequently relieved of his command.

MacArthur later would speak around the country about socialism and communism, corruption in government and in politics and about the taxes people were burdened with. He died April 5, 1964.

Fred, Goldie's husband, was in Japan at the end of the war. He had followed Jamie everywhere the 13th went. When he was in the service, he was there when General Yamashita came out of the woods and was instrumental in his capture. Yamashita was dressed in his best uniform when he was captured.

The first part of December 1952, Jamie said goodbye to all her acquaintances and family in the States. When Jamie arrived in Japan, she was quite anxious because of the horrible things that were done in World War II to our men but she would never have a bad experience while living in Japan. She found the Japanese were very polite to Americans. She thinks they were nice to them because they accepted their defeat in the 2nd World War because of their belief in fate. It was simply their fate to be defeated.

The Occupation ended in 1952 but the treaty of Mutual Co-operation and Security gave the United States the right to maintain military bases in Japan.

Jamie believes there are only bad leaders and most people are nice anywhere you go. The Japanese had started the war with the United States because they needed oil and wanted also to be number one in the balance of power in the world. At the time the United States and Japan were both number one and this to the Japanese way of thinking upset the order of things. One had to dominate over the other.

Jamie lived in the nurse's quarters, which were very small. The rooms were so small you could touch both walls when in bed. She slept on an Army cot with a thin mattress. At least they had privacy. Jamie and the other nurses lived across a bridge from the Sumo wrestlers. Sometimes when walking across the bridge she could see them through the big windows and thought it was fascinating.

Sumo wrestling is the Japanese national sport. It is an ancient sport legend says began in 712 AD. In the Kojiki, which is the oldest book in Japan. It is recorded possession of the Japanese islands was determined by two men who fought on the shores of lake Izumo. Takemikazuchi won the battle and the islands were ceded to the Japanese people. Takemikazuchi established the imperial family of which the present emperor claims his ancestry. Each Sumo match is a recreation of this history. The objective in Sumo is to toss your opponent out of the ring. At the beginning of the match they toss salt to purify the ring. The ring is blessed by a Shinto priest before and after a battle. The Sumo wrestlers are enormous in size. The heavier they are, the harder it is to force them out of the ring. Their bouts only last a few seconds. Sumo is really mental warfare - the art of winning before a first move is made, so they stare at each other to try to break the opponent's concentration. Injuries are rare but there is a lot of slapping, to break the opponent's concentration, pushing and tripping along with the body throws. To Jamie's surprise, a lot of women loved to watch Sumo.

Jamie was assigned as Head Nurse in the Neuropsychiatric Ward at the United States Army Hospital March 1, 1953 until February 28, 1954. She was assigned to the Durbuing hospital as Head Nurse of a Closed Male and also the Women's Neuropsychiatric Ward. She assigned, directed and supervised all the professional and non-professional nursing personnel working on this ward. She assisted the ward officer in carrying out prescribed patients treatments. She assumed the leadership of the nursing team in carrying out all the patient's care and maintaining ward discipline. She also was coordinator for interdepartmental services in the effective management of the patients. She contributed valuable improvement ideas for the nursing service. She was immensely tactful and skilled in her knowledge of people and her self-preparedness earned the respect of her co-workers and supervisors. This facility was in direct support of the Korean operations of the troops who were stationed at and fighting the Korean War in South Korea.

In Jamie's Leisure Time, she explored Yokohama. She saw the women going along the Ginza when she went to buy food sometimes in the evenings. They were wearing kimonos and getas, which are wooden shoes. They would bow as they went by and giggle to each other. But, as a whole, Japanese women were adopting American ways. They had won new freedoms and were outwardly showing it by their dress. They, for the most part, wore dresses and walked with their boyfriends holding hands now. In a few short years, the presence of Americans had changed their way of life in so many ways.

The houses were all built of wood and very small. There were dirt roads almost everywhere. Trucks driving by would rattle the walls and everything in the houses. When there were earthquakes, it was the fires that destroyed so much because all the houses were wooden.

When she got to Tokyo, Jamie went to the Military Post Exchange as it was called, and she met all the people she had known at Ft. Monroe. She couldn't go to the Commissary or Post Exchange without running into someone she had known there.

In exploring the Ginza, searching for little presents for her nieces, she enjoyed the sights and sounds of the little shops and people on the streets. All her gifts were unusual, especially the Kokeshi dolls that were hand-carved and came from every Prefecture in Japan. The shopkeepers all had a nice custom of giving gifts when you made a purchase. One storeowner gave her one dozen purple chrysanthemums when she bought a big vase. She was amazed at this custom and often came back to this store. The chrysanthemum is the Imperial Japanese flower.

She also found the Japanese were very kind and sensitive people. One time when she was lost in Tokyo, a man walked with her and some friends for 4 blocks to show them where they needed to be, taking time out from his busy schedule.

It surprised her to see a beautiful Japanese woman dressed in a very expensive kimono coming out of a small house. Japanese women prided themselves on always looking good and spent a fortune on kimonos. It amazed Jamie how they could walk on their high wooden block shoes.

Jamie observed two teenage boys playing Kendo. She was caught up in that moment watching them. They were attacking each other with a fascinating pattern of footwork and skill with the long bamboo poles. With each swing strike they would shout. She was reminded of what she had read about the Samurai of old, and that this was a martial arts that derived from swordsmanship of the Samurai when they maintained order in Japan in the 9th to 19th centuries.

Before Jamie left for her new Tour of Duty in Japan, she had a little time to study the Japanese culture. She remembered reading a sign in Times Square that said, "In order to gain the wealth of the Indies, one must take the wealth of the Indies with them." She became a student of the Japanese. She had witnessed first hand the Japanese at war, but in reality living amongst them, she found that they were very polite, warm and kind people. She was fascinated with the study of the Samurai class and realized how important this study was in understanding the Japanese.

The Samurai was the dominant and a once proud warrior class who had a profound effect on the Japanese people, in their government and in their thinking, their business, customs, rituals, sports, characteristics and habits, in all aspects of their life. As an island nation, their culture has been in the past very insular and free from outside influence, except for the Chinese influence in the early history of Japan. Being an island nation they developed their own uniqueness as a people. The Samurai Code is embodied in Bushido, the way of the warrior. Bushido is the soul of the Japanese people. In the way of the warrior, there are two kinds of principles, with four levels. The Code teaches one about bravery, loyalty, duty and honor. To always be mindful of death, this keeps one more attentive to people and responsibilities. If people do not honor their parents they are not good people. Even with strangers it is correct to be attentive if they have shown you a kindness.

Traffic was not the problem it would become years later, and she could get around freely or hitch a ride in an Army jeep before she got her brother to ship the car to her. The Japanese drove very fast and she was wondering if she really wanted to drive.

Not only was the traffic fast and unpredictable, they drove on the left side of the street. This in itself was a hard lesson to learn quickly. Japanese men were afraid of American women drivers because their women didn't drive. It seemed to them American women were really aggressive on the road and they definitely didn't like it because their women were so subdued.

Japanese men were in a hurry all the time. It was like being on a speedway every day of your life and Jamie wondered how they could keep it up. They were highly nervous people to start with and the traffic must have driven them into a frenzy on a daily basis. There were a lot of people getting around on bicycles, which looked very risky at best. The traffic made it a very noisy affair.

On several weekends, Jamie ventured out of her area with friends to explore. She took the train to Zushi, and to Kamakura where the big

Buddha is. The Buddha statue there was called Daibutsu or Great Buddha. It was cast 750 years ago. This was in the Kotoku-in-temple. It is said a tidal wave destroyed the temple that had covered it. It is eleven meters tall. It withstood the great earthquake in 1923. It was a very impressive statue.

She traveled on the efficient trains to all points north, south, east or west. The trips were fascinating, watching the Mama sans from the train window washing their beautiful silk kimono material in the huge rivers, seeing the lovely ancient castle like homes on the verdant and lush green hillsides and old wooden houses perched on hills. Zushi was one of her favorite destinations. There were a myriad of old shops and the antique dealers were numerous. The Japanese sold their antiques for a pittance because they wanted everything new and American. Jamie found a wonderful little Yakitori restaurant there.

On a day off one day, Jamie was in Yokohama and walking with a Japanese man who was showing her directions to some place and a Japanese man passing them by said, "Look at that woman with her Japanese lover!" He didn't realize Jamie could speak the language. Not many Japanese spoke English and not many Americans spoke Japanese, so communication was a little difficult, but Jamie, in preparation for her being stationed in Japan had taken a crash course in the Japanese language. She didn't get to interface with many Japanese but those with whom she did were very nice to her.

Jamie in her spare time went to Sophia University in Tokyo in the evenings, which was about half an hour away. She studied English and The History of Western Civilization, Philosophy, and Advanced Nurse Administration #1, working for her BA degree.

Jamie had been to a party one evening and was disturbed by what some of the nurses said. So many of the nurses didn't care for dependents, dependents were the wives and children (up to age 20) of military men, or spouses of military women. They thought the dependents were spoiled and unnecessary. Jamie couldn't take that, and said, "Don't say that about them! They are important to our troops." Her conversation was overheard by the chief nurse of the Far East.

The chief nurse contacted Louise Roskowitz and told her about the situation and Louise told the chief nurse, "I know Jamie loves children and she would be perfect for the job as school nurse." They needed a health nurse out in Yokohama and so they asked her if she would go.

✿ ✿ ✿

As a school nurse, and now a captain, she was stationed first in Tokyo and then went to Camp Drake. Jamie was nurse to Camp Yokohama Dependent Schools System, which consisted of five schools. Enrollment consisted of 1,850 students. She worked under the supervision of the Camp Surgeon. Her duties were to supervise the school health program and she conducted a health education program in all the schools. One was a High School, another a kindergarten at Camp Magill in Yokohama. She was nurse to first and second grades also. Most of the students were Navy dependents. She loved children and enjoyed her duties at the schools. Her usual duties were to check ear, nose and throat and make sure they had all their shots. She was responsible for their school lunch menus in coordination with the school nutritionist. She made sure they got enough water to drink and didn't get dehydrated. She prescribed two play times a day for 15 minutes each and a half hour nap on their tatami mats for the kindergarten, first and second grades. It was an easy job after the horrendous scenes she had seen in New Guinea and the Philippines.

Some of her duties were instructing and supervising responsible people in home care in the prevention and control of communicable diseases and personal hygiene. She obtained help for physiological and psychological problems affecting the school children by referring them to welfare agencies.

Jamie was well liked by associates and by the children. She was very original in planning programs and efficient in carrying them out. She was assigned to this billet as School Nurse from March 6, 1954 to May 23, 1954, and in this short time she accomplished much.

Japanese love parades and there is a parade for almost every occasion one can imagine. The one most enjoyed by the Japanese children was the End of Summer Parade. There were three big bare breasted men with Japanese Sumo skirts on and scarves on their heads beating wildly on huge Taiko drums. The Taiko Drummers were sitting on flatbed trucks and one person was throwing candy to the children. They would beat on those huge drums during the entire parade. Jamie so enjoyed watching the rosy-cheeked happy Japanese children running behind the truck picking up the candy.

Any excuse for a festival or parade is occasioned almost each day. Most are Shinto and mark agricultural cycles, and historic events of local towns.

Some are dedicated to sewing needles and silkworms. These festivals, which mean, worship, also include sacred dances.

One of the festivals Jamie enjoyed was the Bon Adori or Obon celebration. It is the adulation of, and the return of their dead ancestors. It is a happy occasion because the Japanese believe they are reunited with their deceased ancestors on that day. Jamie and her nurse friends joined in the dancing and Jamie felt akin to the Japanese even though she was a Gaijin or white devil. Gai means "outside", Jin means "person". Meaning someone different from us, from a different country, a different race or different in thinking. But in actuality we are all human spiritually and physically. The performers of the dance were on a stage with the paper lanterns swinging suspended from the top of the stage frame, the Japanese dancers were dancing for the crowd to the music of the Taiko drums and Japanese orchestra music. From, two year olds, barely able to walk, to old Mama sans dancing to the music. The Japanese dancers on stage were very masterful dancers, moving in an undulating very sinuous and flowing manner. They did the Coal Miner's Dance or Tanko Bushi, the fan dance, and many others.

In observance of this holiday there is a flurry of cleaning and getting rid of the old and bringing in the new with a fresh new clean house. They place fruit and vegetables on tables for their ancestors. People go to their ancestors' graves and paper lanterns are hung outside their homes to bring their ancestors spirits back home.

Another notable festival is the Cherry Blossom Festival, an old traditional festival signaling the first sign of spring.

The Coming of Age Festival was a fairly new national holiday declared in Japan in 1948. It's a fun filled day, but also one of advice given to young people becoming adults.

✿ ✿ ✿

Operation Dependent Rescue

When Jamie was a Public Health Nurse, she took a group of teenage Dependent children on a summer camping trip. They went by bus to Lake Matusu close to Mt. Fuji. After they had been there a few days, the Army asked her if she needed emergency help but she never did. The young ones got a little homesick and Jamie spent a lot of time comforting them. They all waited in their tents, waiting for her to come and give them a hug or a pat. One professional scout, one WAC and Jamie who was the nurse, and a couple of enlisted men and several Japanese were sent on the trip. She said she should have to enforce two things: a head cover or caps as protection against the sun during the day, and a nap after lunch, otherwise she didn't think they'd have any problem. She took them on hikes for about one hour into the woods and back, and they carried canteens full of water and a snack of an apple or tangerine to eat along the way. It seemed they were always hungry. They had come to the camp with changes of clothing and rain gear. Jamie had her hands full trying to keep track of where they all were. They finished the two weeks, and they didn't have to call for help and then they went back to Tokyo. Then Jamie got a second contingent of another 120 children.

They had been there only three days when a typhoon hit. Jamie was worried one of the tent poles would fall and hit them because they couldn't keep the tent pins in. The wind would come in and they would just whip the pins out. So she said, "Why don't we move all these kids into one tent? They will be crowded but they will be warm."

Jamie, realizing the dangerous situation that was unfolding, said, "I think we'd better call camp Fuji and have them send some trucks to get these kids out of here."

So Jamie called camp Fuji and asked for 6 trucks and 2 men with each truck but they lost one truck coming up. They finally got them up there. Jamie asked if it was still safe to go down that night. She was told they couldn't guarantee anything. Despite that, Jamie knew it was time to get all 120 girls organized. Once she got them all together Jamie said, "Let's load everyone in the trucks, back to back so they will be warm." They were, quite a motley looking crew, some had on night gowns, and some had shirts and slacks on, but they all got off that mountain safely.

Jamie walked into the commanding officers office at Camp Fuji and he started laughing and couldn't stop. Jamie said, "This may be funny to you, but it isn't funny to me. I know what I look like." She looked very motley in her strange combination of attire very un-military! As a fairly new Army nurse she normally was always squared away, clean cut and nicely dressed.

Her hair was long in those days, down to her waist, so she had rolled it up and put a shower cap on and that had popped up to the top of her head. She had on a sports jacket and slacks left over from WWII. In those days the colors weren't permanent so they ran and they were multicolored. She had on a pair of Red Joyce shoes and the water she had been in all night had loosened the soles and they were flapping. Finally, he stopped laughing and said, "It just so happens that I have an empty mess hall. I'll have them put the heat on and I'll arrange to have cots put in and blankets and send in a cook crew and prepare some food." They were at Camp Fuji two nights and for six meals there. Then they set off down the mountain. The girls started telling Jamie they were hungry. There were quaint little Japanese teahouses half way down the mountain. Jamie knew they didn't have much money, so she said, "We can get you soup or tea, but not much more." The girls were good sports about this even though they were very hungry.

Finally the trucks resumed their trip and took them from the teahouse to the train station. They had to change trains halfway to Tokyo. It was rather hectic keeping track of all the girls on the train with the trains taking off in a split second, it was a mad dash for all to get on board and be accounted for. Jamie and her aide, Barbara, had spent their money and got them to Tokyo without anything happening to any one of them. What a relief to have them all safely home again.

When school started, Jamie was back as school nurse and the kids who had been on that trip were the talk of the school.

Jamie's tour in Japan was winding down and she was going to find it very difficult to leave the children she had become so fond of. The kids loved her and they would come running towards her when they saw her. They gave her a woodblock print they had bought as a going away present when she left Japan.

Jamie was reluctant to leave the Orient, she had many happy memories there, and many friends, especially the children, but it was time. Duty called.

✻ ✻ ✻

It was Christmas and Jamie was back in the States living in the San Francisco Bay Area. Jamie loved to spoil her nieces with presents from the Orient, silk jackets with dragons on them, parasols made out of rice paper and all sorts of intriguing treats. She loved telling her stories and showing slide shows of places she had been to her fascinated audience of nieces.

CHAPTER 13

Letterman Hospital

Jamie was assigned to Letterman hospital on January 28, 1955 and promoted to Head Nurse of the Neuropsychological Ward at Letterman. Her tour of duty at Letterman hospital would be from January 28, 1955 to August 1, 1958.

Some of her duties at Letterman as Head Nurse were preparation and administration of medications, including narcotics. She kept meticulous notes on the patient's behavior and was keenly aware of changes in a patient's condition. She assisted the medical officers with their treatments and diagnostic procedures. She also supervised the ward personnel. She was Head Nurse of an unusually large closed psychiatric ward. She displayed great professional growth at this time and performed her duties with firmness, dignity and great insight. She worked hard and was forceful and energetic in her duties. She strove to improve the performance of her staff along with her own.

Jamie was now a mature woman and in command of every situation she was faced with and not discouraged, upset or confused in the face of any difficulties. She was quick to grasp situations and extremely interested in all aspects of her duties as Head Nurse. Her hallmark was her kind understanding of her patients and the way she inspired confidence in both her patients and personnel. She volunteered many hours of her own off-duty time to carry out special treatment plans for her patients.

She was living in quarters at this time and the TV room was just outside her door. People would be in there all night watching television so she enrolled at Sofia University. She decided she needed her own apartment. She rented an apartment with two bedrooms with a friend. It wasn't too far from Kaiser hospital and they could see part of the Golden Gate Bridge from their window. When they looked straight ahead they could see the Civic Center.

Jamie went to San Francisco State College in the evenings and took Economics, Geography, Social Science and Mental Health. She was working for her degree in Nursing Education.

Shortly after she came back from Japan, Father Quinan, who baptized her in New Guinea into the Catholic faith, moved to nearby Calistoga. She went up to see him at the Easter Vigil, which is a mass celebrated after sunset on Holy Saturday, the night before Easter and he was there. He almost passed out when he saw her, and he said "Happy Easter, would you be able to cook breakfast for me? Then I can let my housekeeper go and be with her family." Well, Jamie thought anyone can fry an egg or make toast, so she fixed his breakfast on Easter morning. When she was getting ready to come back to San Francisco, he told her the members of his church had donated food and her whole trunk was filled. She went back to see him again later and he filled up the trunk again.

CHAPTER 14

San Antonio, Texas

August 5, 1956, Jamie was sent to Texas to Administrative school for classes in Advanced Nursing Administration in preparation for her duties in Germany.

At the administrative school in San Antonio, Texas, Jamie talked to head nurse, Mrs. Beaman, into giving her father a red dachshund from the litter of seven. Her father had wanted a female because he thought they were gentler but she got a male. He was named Kaiser Bill, but he later changed his name to Rusty.

✡ ✡ ✡

On April 1, 1957 Jamie was on her way back to California to serve at Letterman again until August 1, 1958.

When Jamie left for California, she had Kaiser Bill sitting on the front seat with her all the way to Mill Valley, California. Kaiser Bill brought untold happiness to her father who was not well physically and there were tears in his eyes when Jamie arrived with her surprise. Kaiser Bill bound out of the car and right into her father's arms. Kaiser Bill eventually lived to be 14 years old.

At Letterman, Jamie served as Head Nurse of Female and Open Ward Neuropsychiatric Nurse Section and later as Duty Night Supervisor.

Before Jamie went to Germany in 1959, she had brought her Father and Mother out to the west coast from Kansas. She bought a quaint little house in Mill Valley for the three of them. Mill Valley is close to San Francisco, across the bay. Her parents had been living in an apartment and she wanted them close to her. She also found a home for Bert and his wife in Hayward, about 20 miles from Mill Valley. Bert taught at Chabot

College and he started the credit union for that college, just as he had done back in Iowa at the end of the war.

Her Dad lived with them for several years. Jamie's father had just had surgery to have a double hernia repaired and she didn't know he was bleeding. All his life he said it was bothering him. Her dear father died about a year later of a massive heart attack. He had just had dinner. Jamie had been at a concert at church and just returned home, and he said, "Come quick Mother, Jamie, I can't get my breath, and have a squeezing pain in my chest." Jamie kept trying to revive him, but she wasn't successful.

Baby Jamie

Jamie & baby Bert

Jamie & Bert 1925

Jamie & parents 1941

Jamie & mother Nov '58

Jamie & Bert

Jamie

Pearl Jamison

Jamie & Robert

Brother Bert

Nursing school

Fred Stewart

Goldie Stewart

Spadra, Ca

Spadra

Desert training

Jamie in Australia 1942

Australia

Kathryn MaryAnne Rose Meyer, Dorothea
Ernst, Pearl, Jamie, Helen Harrick at Ft.
Monroe

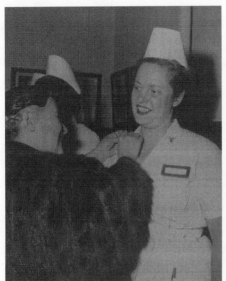

Major Jamie

Japan 1950

Cardinal Spellman and Jamie

Jamie before Vietnam

Jamie's tent Vietnam   93rd Evacuation Hospital, Vietnam

Nurses in Vietnam   Mortar attack

Photo: US Army - UH1 Huey

Photo: US Army – UH1 Huey

Photo: US Army – UH1 Huey

Photo: US Army – UH1 Huey

93rd Evacuation Hospital, Vietnam

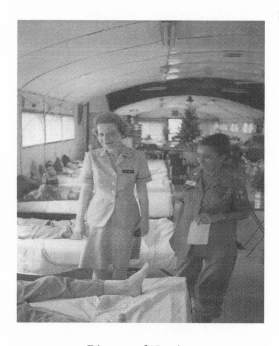

Director of Nursing

Baby Jane

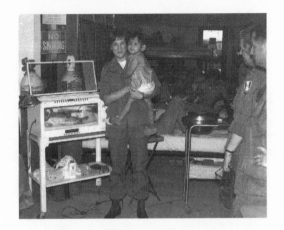

Ward at the 93rd

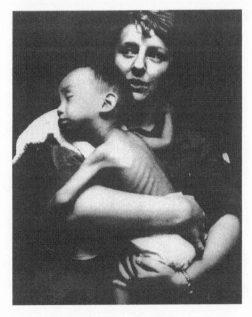

Nurse and child

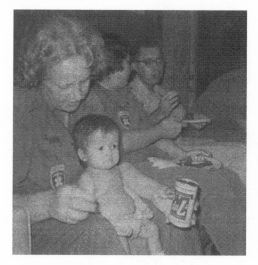

Jamie & baby Jane

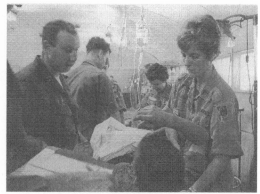

On the ward

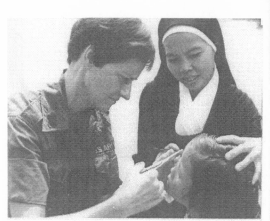

Medcap

Orphanage children

Singapore

Jamie after Vietnam

Coming home from Germany

Letterman San Francisco

Retirement, 1967

Retirement ceremony

Glenna Goodacre, Sculptor

Memorial Dedication

Rolling Thunder

Jamie, Diane, Jane & Rolling Thunder

Jamie and Diane Evans

Memorial

10th Anniversary

Memorial night ceremony

The Wall

Wildwood cabin

Memorial Poster

Jamie & Author

Rolling Thunder Pentagon Parking Lot "The Run"

Vietnam Women's Memorial

CHAPTER 15

Europe during the Cold War

What's this We business?

The Cold War began just after World War II and it ended when the Berlin wall was torn down in 1989.

In the Second World War, the United States had allied itself with the Soviet Union to defeat Japan and Germany. The Soviet Union suffered badly in the Second World War trying to protect its European borders. After the war, in 1946, Winston Churchill warned the world about the Iron Curtain, as he called it, descending on Poland, Bulgaria, Czechoslovakia, Hungary, Yugoslavia, East Germany and Romania.

The Unites States tried to stop the growth of communism in Western Europe with the Truman Doctrine to help countries threatened by communism. This doctrine was instrumental in stopping communism in Greece and Turkey. Also implemented was the Marshall Plan that strengthened the economies and governments in Europe.

Germany was in the midst of this conflict. The Soviet Union had blockaded surface transport of supplies into West Berlin in 1948. In order to provide supplies to these peoples, President Truman ordered military planes to fly in food, medicine, and coal for over a year with planes landing every three minutes. This was called The Berlin Airlift. Later, in 1949, the blockade was lifted. Many believe this action of the airlift prevented a third World War.

NATO was formed that same year to defend against Russian forces in Europe, especially to keep them out of West Germany. Tensions increased and the Soviet Union provided political and economic influence in Asia and the United States then created the Southeast Asia Treaty Organization, SEATO. In the 50's, the Unites States sent military advisors to Vietnam to defend itself from the North Vietnamese. This would escalate into the Vietnam War.

In June of 1950, North Korean forces crossed the 38th parallel and invaded South Korea. Five days later Truman authorized the use of American ground forces to repel the invasion of South Korea. The war would last for three years, ending in July of 1953. Nearly 25,000 American soldiers were killed and more than 100,000 were injured in that war. More than a million South Koreans and more than a million Communists lost their lives.

✿ ✿ ✿

Jamie got her degree in Liberal Arts from San Francisco State University. On the move again, she was en-route to Germany on March 10, 1959. She had been to New Guinea, Japan, Australia and the Philippines and now she wanted to see the other side of the world.

As soon as Jamie received her orders, her mother wanted to go with Jamie. Jamie said, "What's this WE stuff? Are you planning on going with me?" Her mother knew all of her friends. She said to Jamie, "It just wouldn't be the same without you here."

Jamie knew it was going to be lonely for her mother. So she decided they would go to Europe together.

Her mother said, "I'm afraid of going by boat, and I'm also afraid of flying."

Jamie said, "How do you expect to get there? You're going to have to go one way or the other."

So she replied, "Well, if you're flying, I guess I will go with you." Since the Army was sending people by plane only, this was their only option.

They took a roomette on the train from San Francisco to Kansas City to take her Dachshund to her sister-in-law and brother Robert to keep for her while she was in Europe. Jamie slept in the top bunk in the roomette on the train with the dog, and the porter would let her know when they came to a stop to let the dog out. Robert had three daughters, one with juvenile diabetes whose name was Suzan. They loved the dog, and immediately dressed the dog in doll clothes. While Jamie and her mother were in Germany, Esther's family made a video as a Christmas gift.

When they returned from Europe several years later, the dog just flew into Jamie's arms and only wanted to see Jamie and her Mother.

Jamie had ordered a Mercedes in advance of their trip to Europe, and it was waiting for them in Germany.

This tour of duty for Jamie would be the highlight of Jamie's life, as it was for her mother. Her mother was very proud of Jamie. Her own mother had to drop out of school when she was very young. Now her own daughter had graduated from college and had a wonderful career in the Army Nurse Corps.

Jamie's tour was three years in Frankfurt, Germany from April 9, 1959 to July 13, 1962. Her tour there was extended a year because there was always a threat during this cold war period.

When Jamie first arrived in Germany, they told her the first thing she had to do was make sure her mother could get out of there in case the Russians made the living tough. Her mother did a practice escape drill from Germany along with some other dependents into France.

The Berlin wall was built on the night of August 13, 1961. A second wall was built in 1962 to keep East Germans from fleeing to West Germany.

On June 26, 1963, President Kennedy was cheered by more than a million West Berliners, when he gave his famous speech "Ich bin ein Berliner." (I am a Berliner). He said, "All free men, wherever they may live, are citizens of Berlin." Kennedy was also cheered by a small group of East Berliners from their side of the wall. He was criticizing movements that try to combine democratic and Communist elements. He also said, "If you think we can work with the Communists, let them come to Berlin." It would be a short five months later President John F. Kennedy would be shot by an assassin's bullet in Dallas, Texas. An entire nation mourned. In 1964, General Douglas MacArthur died. In 1964 Communist boats attacked U.S. ships in the gulf of Tonkin, southwest of Hanoi Vietnam. The U.S. Senate and House of Representatives voted to give President Johnson authority to strike back against the Communists in North Vietnam.

One day Jamie was leaving for work and spotted something blue on the ground and thought it was a toy a child had left. On closer look, she discovered it was a bluebird on the ground. To her surprise, it jumped up on her finger and she carried it into her house. She found a cage for it and he became a permanent resident for their entire tour in Germany. Her mother would let the little bird out of his cage when Jamie came home from work and he would fly onto her neck and cuddle. One day she came home, her mother was crying and Jamie thought someone in the family had died. The little bird, that was really a member of the family, had flown out of the cage, flew into a table, landed on her mother's lap and died there. Her mother was inconsolable!

Her Mom walked to the PX, which is the Post Exchange, or store, from the quarters. She would buy many teapots for friends, family, and cats and pottery dogs. They wound up getting rid of them all when they moved back to the states. Her Mother used to tell everyone about being Jamie's dependent, "I'm the oldest Army brat around here!"

Jamie was in charge of the entire psychiatric ward. She had attained significant power and rank and she was where she wanted to be, and she had her mother with her.

Jamie's rank in Germany was Major in 1957. As Supervisor of the Psychiatric wards, she was Superintendent of the Psychiatric Dept. in Frankfurt, Germany at the 97th General. This highly competent nurse always performed her duties in a superior and tactful manner and always remained calm when under pressure from the unpredictable patients. She was very understanding of the psychiatric patients and their needs. But when necessary, she could be pleasantly firm. She was now very self-reliant and completely dependable at all times, she maintained a pleasant atmosphere within the unit by her ability to work harmoniously with others. She counseled her personnel and her neuropsychiatric specialists. She was Psychiatric Supervisor for the women's floor and the men's floor. Because of her excellent managerial ability, her portion of the nursing load in the hospital was run extremely well and required very little corrective supervision. She was always keenly aware of her patients needs and her patients appreciated their splendid nursing care and the good morale of the personnel.

The work was easy for her and, as a result, she was getting a little bored. She felt as if she was like a plane in a holding pattern. Even though she was in charge of a very large group of nurses, she had the capabilities to handle a much bigger facility with many more patients.

In Jamie's evening hours she took courses at the University of Maryland, Europe division, to complete her Bachelor of Science degree in 1957. She also utilized her off duty time to prepare speeches of lesson plans covering many subjects to present to her enlisted personnel. She had extraordinary communication skills in both oral and written speech. She kept up to date on professional data and world data.

At Christmas, they always had two important people visit them at the hospital, Cardinal Spellman and Bob Hope. Bob Hope had started his Christmas tour in Berlin, Germany in 1948 during the Berlin airlift. In 1956, when Jamie was stationed there, he came to the hospital to entertain the patients and each year he was there at Christmas to entertain. He was always Jamie's favorite comedian. Cardinal Spellman was always there at

Christmas also. It wouldn't have been Christmas without Bob Hope and Cardinal Spellman visiting the hospital.

Jamie's mother was a fabulous cook. The kitchen was always full of newly baked pastries and at Christmas she really pulled out the stops and made cinnamon twists, prune rolls, fudge, and all sorts of cookies and candy. The house was always full of friends. Even though Jamie and her mother didn't have their family with them, they had their adopted family of friends and Christmas was a truly wonderful time at these two Jamison's.

Jamie and her mother were on the road at every chance they had for time off. They traveled to fourteen countries during Jamie's tour of duty in Europe. One of their special trips was to Italy, where they visited Florence, Venice and Rome. Though they were robbed in Milan when they went to see the Last Supper, it was a special time.

They drove all over Italy and when they went to the fountains of Trevi, her mother said, "Stop the car. I have got to throw some coins into the fountain so I will have good luck and come back to Italy!"

It was a dream come true to live in Europe for Jamie and it was the highlight of her life and of her Mother's and they had four years of living a wonderful life in Germany.

CHAPTER 16

Ft. Polk, Louisiana

After Jamie came back from Europe to the states, she was stationed for a few months in Ft Polk, Louisiana, at U.S. Army Hospital from October 16, 1962 to April 14, 1963. The station hospital was very historic. It had been there since the Civil war.

Jamie was Head Nurse at the US Army Hospital at Ft. Polk.

The summer after Jamie got back from Germany, Jamie invited her niece Esther to come for a visit. Jamie and Esther went fishing off a dam and caught a ton of fish but the fish were so bony you couldn't eat them.

✫ ✫ ✫

From Ft. Polk Jamie and her mother went to Brook Hospital in San Antonio, Texas. The two of them were off to San Antonio where Jamie had been stationed before she left for Germany. Brook Army Hospital was one of the biggest hospitals in the country.

When they arrived July 8, 1963, Jamie's Mother saw some beautiful houses and wanted to live in them. Jamie said, "Those are for very senior officers." Jamie rented a small three-bedroom house where she could see the San Antonio lights at night. They had banana trees in the backyard.

Esther and her sister flew down to San Antonio and stayed with their Auntie Jamie while their parents went to an International Barbers convention. Her younger sister Suzan died when she was 14 years old in April 1949. Esther was the daughter of Robert, Jamie's oldest brother who was 10 years older than Jamie.

Jamie went to see her dear brother Robert when he was ill. He was 54 years old. His untimely death was a result of a brain tumor from an accident with a semi truck. He was in the Veteran's Administration

Hospital in Kansas City. A blood clot broke from his leg and went to his heart.

San Antonio was one of Jamie's favorite duty stations. She served there until December 17, 1964 as Neuropsychiatric Supervisor.

✿ ✿ ✿

Her next duty station would be Letterman Hospital in California again, and on January 6, 1965 she reported for duty. She served in the capacity of Educational Coordinator, in the office of Chief Nurse. Her main specialty was Psychiatric Director and at this time she held the rank of Major.

When they moved back to California, she discovered new tenants had moved into her Mill Valley house. They had three little children and Jamie said to her mother, "I can't ask them to move out," so they found a house in Corte Madera to live in.

During this time America was involved in South Vietnam. Letterman's staff had a complement of 1,090 officers and enlisted personnel and 735 civilian employees. The new hospital cared for over 900 in-house patients each month. The outpatients numbered more than a half million. Prior to this duty station, Jamie donated money to the construction of this hospital and had been asked for advice on its design.

At this time, the war protestors were out in large numbers, protesting the Vietnam war and there was much chaos in the streets in Berkeley and Oakland in California as well as across the nation. Jamie would soon be sent to Vietnam herself. She volunteered and she was en-route to Vietnam November 6, 1966.

CHAPTER 17

Vietnam

Arriving in Saigon

"This is not a jungle war, but a struggle for freedom on every front of human activity."
- Lyndon B. Johnson, 1966

Arriving in Saigon at 4:30 am, 29 November of 1966 was unsurpassed in sight and sound. The sky was lit by flares and artillery fire and smelled of napalm. There was little doubt they were in the middle of a war zone. There were no hills in this area of Vietnam, only flat land. Nam they called it. You could see for miles. All the time there was action close by, constant mortar attacks. There was a surreal foreboding quality about the land. There was the pungent odor of the steaming jungle and the relentless heat, where the temperature never dropped below 90 degrees all year long. Danger was always very close at hand and Jamie was acutely aware of being in a combat zone. This was her new Tour of Duty.

Young Vietnamese men were sleeping on the base floor at the entrance to the billet where Jamie was taken to spend the next few hours. Later that morning she was taken by jeep to Long Binh where she was assigned as the Chief Nurse of the 93rd Evacuation Hospital. Although this was her third war, she was shaken at the sight of our fine young wounded men who reached the hospital by helicopter, less than an hour after taking fire. It seemed no one had only one wound. Her first task was to find the wounds and treat them appropriately.

Jamie was quite definitely a real life action figure nurse, now on duty in Vietnam with the significant rank and power of a Lt. Colonel. She had 20 days en-route to visit relatives and she arrived in Vietnam in Khaki trousers, short sleeve shirt and combat boots. She was ready to go to work.

Jamie had volunteered to serve in Vietnam because she was afraid some of the young new nurses wouldn't be able to handle the problems that might occur. Jamie was a take charge person. She was mindful of the captain in New Guinea who had committed suicide and the shock it had been to all her fellow nurses. Her heart went out to all nurses who served. Jamie was openhearted, stalwart, and open-eyed, very watchful and discerning in her judgments. She knew some of the nurses wouldn't be able to cope with the problems of living in a foreign land, and, being in a war zone, and she wanted to be there for them.

The younger nurses were also volunteers and most had only had one year of experience and didn't even know how to give an injection. From a practical point of view, she probably taught them most of what they would know to perform their duties as nurses. Not being experienced in diagnoses of the injuries also put a lot of stress on the new nurses. For some it was their first time on the ward. The horrendous wounds, getting used to the smell of blood and trying to focus on their duties to these men was trying for them. It was difficult getting their bearings at first. Jamie was a strong leader and tried to teach them how to deal with these problems. She was now Second Chief nurse of the 93rd Evacuation Hospital at Long Binh, Vietnam, and in charge as Chief Nurse of a 400 bed hospital in a combat zone and responsible for all nursing responsibilities in this command. Her tour of duty was from November 29, 1966 to August 14, 1967. She had just achieved the rank of Lt. Colonel in June 21, 1966. She would be known to the doctors and nurses as Colonel Jamie.

The hospital had only been open for a year. The next closest hospital was in Saigon. The hospital at Long Binh was a huge complex with 10 or so hospital buildings. Four Quonset huts had been placed so the building was in the shape of a cross. Each hut held twenty cots and the nurse's station was in the center so the staff could observe eighty patients. The operating room was small and equipment was WWII vintage, but was quite workable.

Jamie's quarters was a little tent with a parachute over it for shade. It was very close to the nurse's quarters, which was a couple of Quonsets.

After a few months, they received the approval for construction of fixed nurses Quarters. What a happy day it was when they had a ribbon cutting ceremony and were able to move in. The sidewalls were eight feet high with open space above that height to the ceiling and there were flush toilets. The cots were double decked but there were no partitions, hence no privacy. Showers and latrines (bathrooms) were outside. It was an improvement, but they had no air-conditioning.

They were able to get some furniture and kitchen equipment from the Quartermaster for the day room area. Friends and family sent care packages. Jamie's mother who was living in their home in Corte Madera, California sent packages of food and the contents of the packages were shared by all who gathered there. Lasting friendships were made at the 93rd.

Dressed in her short sleeve Army tan and green fatigues and combat boots, Jamie went to work at the 93rd.

During her first days of duty in the hospital, she did not remember having to call for backup help to come to the triage area. They just appeared and stayed until the wounded were cared for. Most were sent to x-ray or the operating room. The operating room was equipped with seven operating tables and one orthopedic table. They only had four orthopedic surgeons and they were very busy. Many times, all eight tables were in use. The nurses were on duty 24 hours a day. Every time they heard those choppers come in, they ran to the hospital. The speed in which they were brought in was a determinant as to how likely it was to make a diagnosis immediately. Mere seconds could save lives. It was imperative to do an operation promptly. The nurses worked zealously, with eagerness, devotion and diligence. They quickly learned all they could about their new jobs. There was no discrimination between the doctors and nurses, they were treated very nicely by everyone.

Jamie was well suited for her job as Chief Nurse with her calm demeanor. She was tough on the outside and gentle and kind and compassionate on the inside. She had huge reservoirs of calmness and strength. But she could be known to raise her voice when she was not being heard and a patient needed immediate attention. Her experience in two wars had toughened her for the tasks at hand now. Minute by minute severely injured men were brought in by helicopter. Her position was in the center of the huge cross of a building with beds going both ways. She could see what was going on in all directions. She was the one who decided where the wounded would be sent, either to triage, or surgery, or to wait until the others had been taken care of. Nothing was routine. Every soldier's injuries were different and it was her job to assess the wounds and what should be done. It was unnerving at best, to hear a grown man scream. They were mortally wounded. The nurses were so busy they didn't have time to even give a few words of comfort to the men. Sometimes the men would die while holding one of the nurse's hands. They were the last person to see them. Their mothers, fathers, wives and family would never see them again. The men whose wounds weren't so bad were dedicated to returning to the battlefield again. They were fighting for their buddies and their country.

Jamie had fifty nurses in her unit and they thought she walked on water. They said she was "…the best Chief nurse." There was an esprit de corps and Jamie called them her kids.

Jamie had a great deal of responsibility. She was in charge of anything that had to do with nursing and medics in this unit. She had some outpatient areas that were staffed by nurses and medics, some satellite areas that Jamie was also responsible for.

Much to Jamie's surprise, she had only been in Vietnam a week and was visiting one of the patients when a bullet came right through the ward. There were double-decker beds in this ward for the men who were recovering from malaria. There was no one in the bed where she was standing. If he had been there, he would have been killed. One morning a nurse began yelling "Incoming, Incoming"! This was their first mortar attack. And to her surprise, all the nurses ran out to photograph the attack.

Jamie yelled, "Get back in the building or in the bunker and get the patients and yourself under the beds!" The Viet Cong had hit the ammunition dump and the fire burned for over 15 hours. Another stray bullet went right by Jamie's leg.

A fellow nurse said, "Boy, you were lucky, you were born under a lucky star." Jamie replied, "It pays to be Irish." The bunker was close and they usually went to the bunker whenever there was enemy fire. This time they had been caught unaware.

✿ ✿ ✿

A very special nurse, named Roberta Gleeson came on board. She had worked a lot of ICU in a civilian hospital. She didn't have a lot of nursing experience, only a couple of years. Jamie didn't usually put new people on the ICU, but they were short and Roberta had civilian experience that qualified her. They worked really hard for 8 hrs. There is a great deal of work done by ancillary people like taking up the IV, etc. in civilian hospitals, and when they got relieved they didn't have to worry, they could do all the other things that needed to be done and prepare for the next shift. In all hospitals, there would be three nurses on the floor. In an Army field hospital all three were exhausted. Actually, all of them were working 12 hours if they were busy but if it were a slow time, they got time off.

As opposed to civilian hospitals, Army field nurses were supposed to stay on duty, wasting their time when it wasn't needed and there were lots of times when they could never get off if they wanted to.

If a nurse looked as if they were being harassed, like some patient was going wild somehow, Jamie would walk through the ward and could calm them. It was as if she had the magic touch. It was amazing what she could do by her mere presence. Everybody respected her no matter what level they were. She was the personification of an Army nurse. She just knew how to handle people and was always calm. It didn't matter how stressful the situation was.

To Roberta, it always meant a lot to see Jamie in church because Jamie enjoyed the faith just as much as she did. Jamie was quiet in her faith. It was her actions that spoke of her goodness.

For Roberta, it was wonderful having someone like Jamie as her mentor. Jamie was the reason she stayed in the Army and would retire eventually as a full Colonel.

She used to work a lot of evenings and they had recorders in the recreation room and a long table for eating together. Jamie came in and usually when she came they were all together.

Roberta took one look at her and said, "My Dad died." Roberta just knew. She would later look back and she'd been thinking about her Dad all through the shift and she just knew he had died. She realized all through this, Jamie was there for her and she made all the arrangements. He had died of a brain tumor.

Jamie made sure she could go on R&R. Roberta was grateful for Jamie, and said, "Jamie made life livable there in Vietnam."

At that time, those in Vietnam were out of touch with the news of the world and didn't realize what was going on at home. Civilians didn't have any idea of what went on over there.

In later years, Roberta felt she did so little compared to Jamie. There were horrendous stories from every war, but just one year in New Guinea was more than what they had.

In Vietnam they were trying to do their best, and people would ask, "Why are you there?" Roberta always felt these guys were being drafted, they had no choice, but somebody had to take care of them. It didn't matter what you felt about the war or anything else, someone had to take care of our men. They were going out there to help people but it got her so mad when she got home. People bad-mouthed the guys who were there. Some were drafted, and some volunteered. One guy she ran into was going for his third tour in Vietnam because he had a kid-brother in the Marine Corps and he didn't want his kid brother being killed. He had what he considered a good job and kept volunteering so his brother wouldn't be called up.

✿ ✿ ✿

The helicopter pilots bunked right by the runway, which was by the entrance to the hospital. The nurses ate meals with the pilots in the chow hall. Jamie always asked them if they had taken fire and almost every day they said they did. Jamie was sitting in the mess hall relaxing for a few minutes one day and in walked Vince who was just back from one of his Hops or Dust Off flights. The jukebox was blaring out some rock and roll music. She asked how he was and he told her, "I took fire today."

Jamie said, "But you aren't wounded." She liked this young man. He was so personable and willing to talk about his mission in Nam. Jamie was a good listener and she admired these brave young men who risked their lives each day to bring in the wounded to her hospital. He started to tell her about his life.

Vince had joined the Marines when he was 18 years old. He had been in Vietnam almost 13 months and his tour of duty was almost over.

He grew up on a farm in Clinton, Ohio. His Dad owned indoor and outdoor theaters. He enjoyed war movies but found in real war it was completely different. He was not prepared for what he would experience during his thirteen month tour of duty in Vietnam. He felt so empty in Vietnam. "I'd move here, move there, it was just an empty feeling. You actually felt like you were in a bottle, and it had a smell, the same smell everywhere in the heat and humidity and rice paddies.

"Until I got acclimated to everything, I had to set my standards on how to get things done, what to do in this situation and what to do in that situation. This took a couple of weeks. It was a culture shock and the biggest thing was you couldn't trust anybody. You couldn't trust the Vietnamese.

"A friend of mine was practicing in artillery practice and accidently killed a Vietnamese man's wife and his oxen. He was fined $350 total, $150 for the wife, and $200 for the oxen. The oxen were more important than the wife because they used the oxen to work their rice paddies."

Vince flew the CH-34 and the UH-1B the Huey.

"On each mission you were scared, but you had to get the job done. With the guys screaming in the back and the corpsman working on them, sometimes I had to put my mind on something else. I'd think about what I had to do, and I'd always take that second to look back to make sure everybody was on, if we had the room. Sometimes we had to go back, up to 10 miles to pick up someone else. Mountain ranges are all north and south, and that was one way if we weren't sure of an area, we just had to look at the mountain range to remember where we were. They were named by their height. We really flew by the seat of our pants until we learned the area.

"We were fired at almost every time we went out. We would get hit. In fact one of the gunners had a hole in his helmet on the first trip out. It spun and flew around and almost fell off."

He was stationed at Johnson City, which was not far from Saigon. The airport had a control tower they called Johnson City International, Elevation 40 feet. "It was a great group of guys. One thing about the Marine Corps, the Marine Corps did not get everything they needed - ever. The Navy got everything! A lot of times if we flew, let's say from Johnson City to 100 miles away, we would use a lot higher altitude to fly from place to place, it was harder for them to get us. They would teach their shooters exactly where to shoot, and how far to shoot at the helicopter. They were very accurate." He also flew a MAG-36 at first and then the Huey. These were gunships. "I picked up people that were wounded and also those that were in body bags and helped put them into the helo, then flew them out.

"One of our gunners came back from a mission with a dead stare. After he got talking he said that he had shot at everything, not knowing who was the enemy or not.

"The men wanted to go back to avenge the death of their buddies - you were fighting for your buddies and also your country. Because, when you got out there, it was helping one another to get the job done and that was in our minds all the time. It was teamwork. Thank heavens it worked really well. One minute you are talking to somebody and the next minute they were hit.

"My helicopter was not the biggest. We had the Jolly Green that pulled up pilots who ejected from the A4's and F4's. They carried an A7 out of the jungle. They look like mosquitoes. They were flat on the bottom, and just had the pilot and co-pilot in it. The Huey carried the troops for drop off. There were 12 to 14 pilots in the squadron. We usually flew 25 miles from the base. There were other bases around that we would use a lot.

"In flying the Huey and the MAG-36, these were both gunships, my mission was to take out the enemy and to defend the wounded I was picking up in the jungle. I always flew over the tree areas, never over water and far enough away from the river area so those on the other side of the river wouldn't actually get at you. When you flew over the wooded area, I'll tell you all the time I was scared, but I did what I had to do. The adrenalin was really going and my hands were numb. When you picked someone up - in their eyes you saw how scared they looked, and how fast they got on the aircraft. And you only had so much time to get the hell out of there. I always took a second look before I lifted up. That was what I always did, because you never knew if there was somebody else that needed to be picked up - a straggler. It just was something I did it to make sure that the job was done. Every mission we flew I got a certificate, but we always got a certificate with name and rank on it."

Jamie said, "I admire all of you helicopter guys. You go right into the field in the midst of all the fighting, pick up the wounded, just minutes after they are wounded and arrive at the hospital a short time later."

"When you heard those helos starting to rumble in, you didn't walk, you ran to the hospital and tended to those bloodied up boys that they brought in." As 'Chief Nurse' and Lt. Colonel, it was incumbent upon her to work harder than everyone else. The helos landed very close to the hospital and the crew carried the men in on stretchers. "I always kept my scissors with me and would run out and cut their clothes and boots off right there and give a diagnosis. We couldn't tell where they were bleeding until we cut off their clothes. It seemed that no one had only one wound. Our first task was to find the wounds and treat them appropriately."

Jamie was known for her calm demeanor in the midst of a tumultuous situation. A battle raged each and every day in the hospital to save lives. She had to choose which men were the worst wounded and send them to surgery immediately. Her decisions were absolute. Life and death dramas unfolded each minute, in rapid succession. She did a diagnosis right there. She checked first for a clear airway, then for a breath, then pulse. Then she'd try to talk to them. Most of the men were conscious but had a great deal of pain.

There was a din of noise and everyone worked in what looked like a highly orchestrated routine, with people running around and making way for the stretchers. They used the ABCDE guide for a quick diagnosis. A is for Airway, to see if there is a possible blockage. B for Breathing, C is for Circulation, D for Disability - most specifically neurological. E - meant Expose. They checked to see if there was anything they had overlooked and if it was catastrophic and needed attention by the surgeon immediately. Then the patient was out of Jamie's hands and the responsibility of the surgeon.

The ICU ward was on one wing. There were two wards for ICU, because there were too many patients for just one ward. The hospital was called Evacuation Hospital, or Evac. They tried to get the patients out the next day. If they were to spend some time in the hospital, they went to Camp Zama hospital in Japan.

Something that must be kept in perspective, is nursing at that time was no touching, don't get involved. Jamie showed, by her example it was okay to hold a patient's hand, to read to them, to do extra little things for them.

One night they were taking Incoming (rockets) and Roberta was working ICU. The patients were getting upset because the nurses had to get them up out of their beds and put them underneath the cots, so their mattresses would act as a cover and protect them. They were really going wild. When one of the patients told Roberta how many springs were in his mattress, she knew he was really in trouble. She ran over to the mess hall and asked for a whole bunch of apples and handed out apples to the patients underneath the beds. She just happened to know these apples came in and she laughed to think how she would explain to people back in the states: You've got a helmet full of apples and you hand them out to these guys because these men were used to having weapons in their hands and being able to fight back. She was saying to them, "You can't fight back, get under the mattress and hold this apple!"

Compared to a lot of places they usually didn't have a lot of attacks, just an occasional bullet or rocket. When you're on the receiving end, and there's a legitimate alert and someone says, Incoming you're scared, because you don't know if it's really coming in or not! They were really fortunate the bullets went flying way over them. They didn't have to do anything but give prayers of thanks.

Some of the psychological wounds the nurses saw would surface later on, maybe years later. Some of the women would never get over some of the sights. Some of the injuries were horrific and frustrating for the nurses because they couldn't be helped. It was difficult on a daily, round the clock basis to cope with suffering and in what time off you had you simply could not block out these sights and sounds of the wounded. It was constant grueling work with no let up. Their minds were on constant alert. Trying to sleep at night was almost impossible, and if they weren't so exhausted, they might not have slept at all. The nurses were duty bound to stick with their patients no matter if they were emotionally on the ragged edge or not. Jamie was the example and she took care of the men with all of her best skills and training ... and all of her heart.

Jamie was also ferociously loyal to her nurses. She was always present in their times of crisis and uncertainty. She had an innate sense of when there might be a problem and she was there at just that right moment. She instilled calmness and positive leadership always.

One of her favorite nurses was First Lieutenant Jenny Morse. Jennie flew into Vietnam on the same plane with Roberta Gleeson. She was very likeable and kind, but she didn't realize how difficult it would be to see the mortally wounded on a daily basis. One day, when she was especially stressed, she said to Jamie, "I don't think I can stand to see another bloodied soldier for another day." Jamie simply said, "You'll do just fine." With this simple statement Jenny was inspired to stay the course of her one year in country in Vietnam. This wonderful nurse would go on with her nursing career and would eventually work for the Veterans Administration in New England.

Jamie certainly led by example. She was responsible for many of her nurses making their careers as nurses a lifetime career, with many retiring at the Lt. Colonel rank. She couldn't talk to anyone about daily problems and kept a lot of that bottled up inside her. She had deep wells of love and an overflowing and constant supply of love for her fellow man. That real mother love asks nothing in return. She cut right through to the heart of a problem and solved it right away. She was tough but she led her staff of nurses and corpsmen with integrity, compassion and wisdom. Because she was a figure of authority, everyone always knew anything they told her would go no further.

One of the men said, "I felt nervous thinking I was flying a million dollar helicopter, and after the first time I was fired at, my baptism of fire, I was thinking the government owed me a million dollars." These men were ferocious, and they were dedicated. Even though it was an unpopular war, this didn't faze them in the line of duty to their country. The helo pilots flying in low and sitting mid-air in plain sight of artillery was a very brave thing. Most of the infantrymen who were wounded were wounded by Claymore land mines they had stepped on. The mines were everywhere and very difficult to detect. A lot of men were missing both arms and legs as a result. Most of the Army brass never did see some of the horrors of war, it was the doctors and nurses who saw these men and tried to get the patients quickly on a plane to Japan.

It didn't matter, if a patient was North Vietnamese, Vietnamese, National or Korean, everybody got the same treatment. The nurses were just there for the patients. One time they were log-jammed and running out of respirators. One of their thoracic surgeons had to take one of the American G.I.'s off the respirator because he was not going to be salvageable. He put the respirator on a Vietnamese who they thought was a communist. Roberta had a fit. She was just boiling. She did all she was supposed to do and it was not something she showed outwardly. You knew in your brain what he was doing was right but her heart and her gut weren't accepting it. This Vietnamese who they had hooked up to the respirator lived, which was a miracle in and of itself. It turned out he was a poet. He was not a North Vietnamese soldier. He was fluent in 4 or 5 languages including English, and he wound up being an interpreter and was just a wonderful man. At the time, Jamie put her arms around Roberta, and said, "This is the right thing, don't worry about it. Everything will turn out right. Everything is okay." Roberta just knew she wouldn't lie to her. Jamie made it possible for her to deal with the unbelievable stress of the moment. It was obvious the man they took off the respirator, even if they had left him on only had an hour or two to live. Roberta was so in awe of all of this. The fact they had a doctor who was so good he could recognize these things. There was so much care for the patient who was taken off the respirator. They put him on Ambubag so he wasn't just left to die. For people like Jamie to come down and make sure she was there and help them at that moment was exceptional.

Those who were sent to the Camp Zama Hospital, the Army hospital in Japan, were the worst wounded and needed a long recovery. Other patients were sent to stateside hospitals close to their hometown. There were a lot of burn patients sent to Camp Zama Hospital. Burn patients suffered agonizing pain. Zama hospital was renowned for their care of burn victims. One of the men was so badly burned he said he wanted to give up, and Jamie said, "You never give up!"

At the 93rd, they also treated Vietnamese civilians. They had one delivery of a baby of a Vietnamese woman who had taken fire to her stomach. Roberta Gleeson, of Beaumont Texas, who was also a midwife, performed cesarean section, and found out the baby had also been wounded by the bullet, before he was born. The supply officer had brought out two incubators several months before and it saved the baby's life.

Jamie would come around every day to see what was going on, how the staff and the patients were and if they had enough beds, because if there were a push, they would transfer people out.

✪ ✪ ✪

Elizabeth Finn had flown in on the plane with Roberta. Elizabeth had been a nursing nun for 18 years before she got out of the convent and became a nurse in the Army nurse corps. Her nickname was Liddy.

She left the convent because she wanted to see if she could pay the bills and do the things everybody else had to do. She really wanted to test herself and she felt whether she succeeded or failed, she would be taken care of. She wanted to test her wings and live independently.

Army life was very structured at Boot Camp and lasted six weeks. The first part of the indoctrination was setting up a hospital, or a quasi hospital and getting used to sleeping on cots and freezing water for showers. For the desert survival course they were taken out into the desert and told to find their way back to camp. There were six people in a group. "Thank God some people knew how to find their way back, I was just along for the ride." It was difficult for Liddy getting used to fatigues and boots after being dressed in a nuns' habit. The usual age for new Army nurses was 20 and Liddy was 36 years old. It was quite a change for her being just out of the convent. She remarked, "They were trying to toughen everyone up and I never thought I got very tough."

She went to Vietnam in 1967. It took 24 hours to get there. The surprise of her life was she thought she'd have a day off when she arrived, but that was a joke. They gave them their uniforms and boots and said, "Tomorrow, you are going to take the place of the head nurse on the Intensive Care Ward who is being rotated back to the states." When Liddy got there she wasn't scared of anything.

Elizabeth was working on the Intensive Care Ward. She had a lot of experience. The group of new nurses who came in from the school of Nursing had graduated in September and didn't really have a lot of experience. It took about 3 months of on the job training in Vietnam to be proficient. They were a lot more creative after that and they took care of the patients in the emergency room. There were several doctors on that ward. The nurses would care for patients that needed sewing up. The wounds had to be dressed and bandages put on. This was all done in the Emergency Room, but when they came to the Recovery Room, they had to monitor blood pressure and pulse, and make sure the I.V.'s were running and change the dressings if they were saturated. The nurses checked to see if there was infection and got proper pain relief. They had to wash the men and feed some if their hands were tied up. They helped them with some things they couldn't do themselves. The nurses were very busy when a lot were brought in at a time.

When the patients were doing a little better they were moved over to the wards. They usually stayed there about 10 days and then they would be ready to be evacuated out to Japan or California. If they were burned they would be sent either to Japan or to Ft. Sam in San Antonio.

There were seven different units or wards, with a total of about 50 nurses on these wards. Elizabeth was in charge of 12 or 15 RN nurses and the medics. The Intensive Care unit had more people because it required more attention. There was a vast difference between what the nurses did and what the medics did. The nurses had a BS in nursing and some had a Masters degree. The Medics were sent through a six month course at Ft. Sam. Most of them had to be trained on the job because they didn't have any professional background.

That once quiet nun had turned into quite a character. Liddy would take her knitting bag, put four cans of beer in it and take it to the older Sergeants, because she thought, A beer would help them recuperate.

One day Liddy was a part of Med Cap in Bien Hoa. The Med Cap or Medical Civilian Aid Program designed to see if children or adults needed medical help at an orphanage which had no doctors or nurses. It was wartime and supplies were not available nor were nurses.

Liddy took the place of a Red Cross woman who was going back to the states for a vacation. She asked Liddy if she would take her place for her and go to the convent because she wanted a continuity of information while she was gone. Jamie made arrangements for a jeep to take Liddy there. The driver parked the jeep outside of the Convent, which was composed of a high wall and inside was a nursery and orphanage. Ordinarily she parked outside the wall, but this time she was asked to move the jeep inside. Later when she returned to the Evacuation Hospital she questioned the movement of the jeep. She told Jamie, and Intelligence questioned her. A short time later it all became clear.

✿ ✿ ✿

The Vietnam War came out of a long fight against the French. Ho Chi Minh set up his Communist party in 1930 with the express purpose of ending the French colonial rule. In 1940 the Japanese occupied French Indo China, and allowed the Vichy French to occupy the Vietnam area.

In 1941 the U.S. stepped in when Japan moved into South Vietnam in search of oil. In 1945 at the end of the war the U.S., in order to get Britain and France out of the area, sided with Ho Chi Minh. The United States, in fact, saved Ho Chi Minh's life. He was very ill with tropical diseases and the OSS parachuted in to take him to a hospital. In September of 1945 Ho Chi Minh claimed Vietnam independent after 80 years of colonial rule. At the same time, the Cold War continued between the US and Russia. The Revolution in China made the US afraid of a Communist Asia. Even with US backing, the French were defeated in the battle of Dien Bien Phu on May 7, 1954 at the hands of General Vo Nguyen Giap, Commander of the Viet Minh. Stalin, fearing a conflict with the US, put pressure on Ho Chi Minh to divide the country. The Stalinists would be given the North, and French the South only with elections so they could decide who would rule Vietnam. North Vietnam became a communist enclave and the US backed the South under the regime of President Diem who was a staunch anti-communist. However, there were no elections. Dwight Eisenhower's aide General Goodpastor claimed if elections were to be held they would give the Communists control of Vietnam. Due to these decisions, war was inevitable. As a result the US gave a great amount of financial aid to the Generals in the South. Fighting between the North and South began in 1956. In 1960, the Viet Cong were established in Hanoi supported by Moscow. The US government feared the domino effect, if Vietnam fell, then all the nations in Asia would fall.

In 1963 the top Generals in Diem's Army plotted a coup and Washington realized the South Vietnamese Army could not defeat the guerrillas alone. America launched its military intervention in Vietnam. On November 1, 1963 Diem's government was overthrown, and Diem was murdered by his own soldiers. All the people in Saigon celebrated Diem's death. President J.F. Kennedy was assassinated just three weeks after Diem's murder and Lyndon Johnson was then in office. He was as strong an anti-communist as Kennedy and ordered the first air strikes on the North.

In 1964 the USS Maddox was on patrol in the Gulf of Tonkin in international waters. It was fired on by North Vietnamese torpedo boats and President Johnson ordered the attack on North Vietnam. Troops landed in Vietnam March 8, 1965. Moscow quickly aided North Vietnam, trying to keep either the US or China from dominating Asia.

✡ ✡ ✡

The first American Marines landed at Da Nang in March 1965 and the first engagement between the US and Vietnamese forces, was November 14, 1965. Secretary McNamara went to Vietnam to assess the damage at a military outpost at Dong Suay, which was destroyed and South Vietnam's expert guerilla troops were killed. McNamara decided after assessing the war that South Vietnam would fall. A huge buildup of troops in the La Drang valley in Central Highlands was the first victory for the North Vietnamese.

Operation Rolling Thunder was a massive bombing operation against the North implemented by President Johnson in hopes this would bring North Vietnam to the Peace Table. Guerilla forces were bringing supplies to the South on the Ho Chi Minh Trail, which connected North Vietnam, Laos and Cambodia. The bombing had no effect on the enemy and as a result President Johnson ordered a huge compliment of ground troops to try to stop the defeat of South Vietnam.

A lot of Vietnamese peasants were lost in the crossfire and it was hard to really tell who the enemy was. The Russians sent thousands of North Vietnamese to the South to fight with the guerillas. As the war went on with no end in sight, the American public was alarmed US forces were taking very heavy losses.

In 1965 the first anti-war rally was held in Washington and eventually over 5 million people across America were involved. As a result soldiers became confused about their missions due to the protests and were skeptical about risking their lives when they, were not backed by their country. They were being led to believe they were fighting an unfair and futile effort to win the war.

North Vietnamese General Vo Nguyen Giap was both brilliant and ruthless. The war had reached a stalemate. He knew he was at a disadvantage in conventional combat because he had been defeated repeatedly by US troops. He had been trained in the tactics of guerilla warfare in his struggle against the French and devised a plan to launch unexpected attacks against US troops. He knew the anti-war movement was growing and he would try to break the will of the American people to win the war.

He had planned a very quick and decisive victory through many attacks. Massive armaments were moved south for an offensive planned on the Vietnamese New Year, which is known as Tet. In the past Tet had been a time of truce in this long war and both Saigon and Hanoi made announcements this year would not be different. The Tet offensive was similar to the surprise attack on Pearl Harbor.

The first attack was on the US Marines' firebase at Khe Sanh, which was in the northwest corner of South Vietnam, close to the Laotian border, with NVA and the NLF staging attacks on South Vietnams cities. Giap had hoped to start a general uprising to encompass the entire country and force America out of Vietnam. In doing so, he had also hoped to affect the election of the US President in 1968.

In 1967 Giap had moved over 20,000 NVA troops into the Khe Sanh area. General Westmoreland reinforced the base with 6,000 Marines, not wanting to repeat the mistakes of the French at Dien Bien Phu.

One of the bloodiest battles took place at this small US Army base. General Giap thought the over-stretched American forces would not be able to protect the base and this would divert attention from the attacks on the big cities. It was a trap and our troops were caught off guard. At dawn January 21, 1968 the first attack began. The battle for Khe Sanh lasted until April 6th with aerial bombings of NVA positions by B-52's and strike aircraft dropping napalm and a multitude of bombs. After fierce battles, Giap's attempt to overrun the base was abandoned. This had served as a diversion.

During the battle for Khe Sahn the General had secret groups of guerrillas going into Saigon and other large cities, undetected.

Like Pearl Harbor, General Westmoreland's staff ignored the intelligence reports something was about to happen. Although General Weyand had put his troops on full alert, there were only a few hundred men on duty the eve of Tet. It was an all out attack on all bases and Saigon and the U.S. Army were taken completely off-guard.

In the following months, the government in Saigon had coup after coup, and if the US Government hadn't supported it, it would not have lasted a week. The war would go on to be America's longest war.

✡ ✡ ✡

Jamie was transferred out of Vietnam before Elizabeth. It was a sad goodbye but Jamie had trained Elizabeth well. She was now fully qualified as an Army nurse.

Another one of the wonderful nurses was Barbara Price. She was a head nurse also and in charge of the POWs.

Another was 2nd Lt. Bev. Bobson. She retired as a full Colonel also.

Connie Kurtley was going to be married to a man she met in Vietnam and she honored Jamie by asking her to be the Mother of the Bride. She asked the captain of the base to be the Father of the Bride.

During Jamie's tour, there were USO concerts at Jamie's hospital. The Corps of Engineers created a little area in the middle of the post and the patients sat on the ground in their blue pajamas with their bandaged arms and legs. The nurses attending them were happy to go to the concerts with the patients.

Bob Hope came to Vietnam usually at Christmas and he entertained there every year from the beginning of the war in 1964 until its end in 1972. His shows had a little vaudeville routine, celebrities, singers, dancers and lots of his off beat humor. Hope said he was "entertaining to remind the troops of what they were fighting for, and a grateful nation cared." Bob Hope came through and the troops loved him and his crew. He brought laughter and a sense of home. Lana Turner came on one of the trips. Phyllis Diller was a great hit with the troops also. Jamie recounted Phyllis Diller had sprained her ankle and she stayed close to Jamie. So Jamie held her hand while the doctors tended to her sprained ankle.

Then Nancy Sinatra came to Long Binh. The nurses who were off duty were the escorts. They watched their patient's IVs. Once the troops heard Nancy Sinatra and her crew, they began yelling and screaming. Roberta wasn't a Sinatra fan at the time but seeing the positive impact Nancy Sinatra had on the troops changed her mind. Suddenly they were teenagers again! When she started singing, "These Boots Were Made For Walking ... One of these days these boots are gonna walk all over you" the troops went hog wild. Later, Roberta thought, you know it was hot out there and those IVs must have had boiling water in them.

When Jamie got orders for R & R, which is Rest and Relaxation in military parlance, she went to the Raffles Hotel in Singapore with a couple of friends. Jamie had always been intrigued by the Raffles hotel. It was a colonial Grande Dame three-story building with high ceilings that looked like an old plantation house. She thought at one point she saw Somerset Maugham peering from behind one of the pillars writing one of his stories. There was the pool with cabanas and an inner court, with inside balconies overlooking the first floor. They ordered a drink and sat by the pool to tranquilize their nerves in that touch of heaven.

The greatest thing about the trip was to sit in a big tub and to get all the dirt off. She couldn't wait to take a bath because the dirt was ground into her skin. When they bathed in Nam, it was just a cold shower with muddy water and they didn't really feel they were clean. They wouldn't have had time for a bath anyway. They were so busy and usually just fell into bed at the end of the day.

Roberta always thought of Jamie as a cross between her aunt and grandmother - the best women in her life.

Everyone was very ethical, honest and caring. The doctors were more businesslike, but the nurses were very compassionate and empathetic. These heroic nurses had that special patient interaction and devotion to them. Jamie said of all the nurses, "I didn't have a bad one in the whole lot."

Jamie made many improvements in the quality of nursing care at the 93rd Evac Hospital. She had with her outstanding leadership motivated the personnel to perform at peak capacity over prolonged periods of time. Amidst the dirt, heat and less than desirable medical facilities, she created a wonderful atmosphere of a completely dedicated patient oriented environment.

Jamie made a trip to the orphanage one day with one of the Red Cross workers to see how the Med Cap program was working. The nurses were so touched by the pitiful condition of the children in the orphanage nearby that they brought clothing, and toys to her office. She was happy to deliver everything to the lonely, dirty and very frightened children. One infant, Jane, caught her attention. She needed all the help Jamie could give her. Jamie found Jane at Long Binh orphanage five miles into town. She was the tiniest thing she had ever seen and had these big sad eyes that just kept looking at her. Jamie's heart went out to her and she picked her up and held her close. She cleaned her, dressed her in new clothes and took her to the hospital to care for her.

One of the nurses told Jamie the children were mistreated and the orphanage people had fed them dog food. Jane would have been dead if Jamie hadn't brought her into the hospital. She was 11 months old and she only weighed 11 pounds. She had anemia. When Jamie brought her into the hospital, a nurse smiled knowingly at Jamie and said, "I know you are going to keep this one." And that was exactly what she did. They started feeding her nourishing food. They kept giving her iron after they built her up physically and finally they had to remove her spleen. She had a clubfoot and they operated on her foot as well. Eventually she got stronger. They had begun calling her their baby. One day a nurse called and said, "Colonel, you'd better get over here, they are going to send Jane back today." Jamie said she would simply not allow it. One of the nurses said, "You're going to take her home with you aren't you?" and

Jamie said, "That's exactly what I'm going to do". The superiors said, "Just take her on the plane with you. There will be no questions asked." Jamie and two other friends adopted her. Jamie is Jane's Godmother. The nurses took in four other Vietnamese children. When Jamie's tour of duty was over in Vietnam, she whisked Jane out of the country and took her home. She wouldn't have lived if she hadn't brought her back to the States.

When Jamie and Jane landed at Travis Air Force Base in the United States, there were carloads of Jamison's relatives there to greet Jamie and little Jane. Her brother, her mother and nieces and nephews came to welcome her home. Everybody was full of love, hugs and kisses. When they got established at home, Jamie's mother and Jamie's newly adopted Goddaughter had a tea party and then she took Jane and her nieces to a nearby circus.

✿ ✿ ✿

The war was unpopular at home. University students were protesting in the anti-war movement. Some of the soldiers said the war shouldn't have happened but there are those who can't agree. They refuse to accept the deaths of their buddies and maintain their having died was worth something.

Most all of the wounds of the men were permanent and some of the worst wounds were not only physical but the trauma of war had affected their minds. It was difficult work for the nurses and it was hard to keep from being sympathetic and remain empathetic and strong for them. Some of the nurses broke down and a few had to be sent home because for some, it was too hard to cope with on a daily basis. Not many Generals or Admirals ever see the horrors of war as these nurses did.

Where did our country get such dedicated and caring men and women? The nurses served as well and as bravely as the combat troops and pilots.

Jamie would remember all these experiences for the rest of her life. "I am glad I was there for the men and the young nurses, but I wouldn't do it again."

Jamie served as Chief Nurse in Vietnam from November 29, 1966 to August 14, 1967.

CHAPTER 18

Retirement

Jamie was a Lieutenant Colonel in 1968 when she was assigned to Letterman hospital, San Francisco, California. This was the last post at which she served. She was Psychiatric Supervisor of the entire hospital and visited every ward on a daily basis. This was her favorite duty station and, as she said to a friend, "I don't know why I had been there so many times. I guess I thought I owned the place!" If someone were in critical condition, she would also visit the patients at night. The new Letterman hospital to be built was on the drawing board and Jamie was involved in those plans. She gave advice on all the operating rooms with consideration of convenience and utilization of space in all rooms and made sure there would be restrooms on every floor for not only patients but for nurses and visitors.

Jamie's love, devotion and selflessness to her family proved very evident when she passed up her opportunity for Bird Colonel because it would have taken her to a duty station in Santa Fe, New Mexico. She wanted to retire with 30 years of service, but this was not to be. The altitude wouldn't have agreed with her mother because she had heart problems, and her mother was always her first concern. So in consideration of her mother, she didn't accept this last assignment. In 1968, after 25 years in the Army, Jamie retired. Jamie had worn many hats, from nurse to Psychiatric Supervisor of an entire hospital working at the 6th Army clinic.

✫ ✫ ✫

It was a cold September morning when Jamie retired in 1968 at the Presidio parade grounds in San Francisco with full military honors, with troops and bands, and trooping the line for inspection. It was a somber day. She was given a certificate of honorable discharge for having served her country so well, after having served 24 years, 11 months, and 28 days of total active service and foreign or sea service 8 years, 1 month and 11 days. This lovely lady Lieutenant Colonel Evangeline Pearl Jamison who had been committed to a purpose greater than herself, was retiring from the service as an Army nurse.

She was the only woman lined up with twelve men. As she stood ramrod straight at attention during the inspection, she thought about how her assignment was fulfilled and she could rest in the knowledge she had done her part for mankind. She thought about all her duty stations in the past, all the patients she had seen and of the friends she had made in all those years. All these thoughts were passing in review as she stood there for her last inspection. She also thought about her favorite president John F. Kennedy and how he had remarked, "The Army was behind this country since George Washington."

Jamie was tired. She had accomplished a lot and she told herself, "There is a time for everything." She had come a long way in her career. She had gone the extra mile. Not many women officer nurses or women officers had been through three wars and lived on four continents and served for 25 years. She was always a standout person and a true leader. She was brilliant, but so humble, a woman of honor and a lady.

She was proud of her accomplishments, but never showed it. She had inspired so many people who had made the Army their career. Some wanted to get out of the Army and Jamie was such a wonderful role model most of her nurses decided to stay in. Many retired with the rank of Lt. Colonel.

The commanding general was checking to see if everyone's boots were spit shined and their uniforms in perfect order.

She was in pain as she stood there at attention on the parade grounds. She had never had her knee taken care of from that old injury long ago in the Philippines. She was always mindful she could be relieved from duty if not physically fit but she was always more concerned about her patients and her family and had never taken the time for her own needs. That was the beauty of Jamie. She loved her patients and family and friends more than herself. A friend had asked her, "Why don't you have that taken care of?" Jamie answered, "You know, I put it out of my mind. I don't know why I didn't have it operated on. I could get around. It hurt a little bit but you get used to it. You get used to pain. I'm just a screwed up Iowan I guess." She would eventually have that right knee and her left hip operated on in retirement and exclaim, "I'm in pretty good shape now, I might even rejoin the Army if they would let me."

✳ ✳ ✳

After 25 years as an Army nurse, Col. Jamison, on her own time, earned her B.S. from San Francisco State college.

For her service as an Army nurse, she was awarded the Legion of Merit for her duties at the 93rd Evacuation hospital in Vietnam, from 1966 to November 1967 for exceptionally meritorious conduct in the performance of outstanding service. She received the World War II Victory Medal; Asiatic Pacific Medal; American Campaign Medal; 3 Over Seas Bars; Korean Service Medal (Oak Leaf Cluster); United Nations Service Medal; Philippine Liberation Ribbon, Philippine Independence Ribbon; Philippine Presidential Unit Citation; Army Commendation Medal (Oak Leaf Cluster); Vietnam Service Medal; also the Republic of Vietnam Legion of Merit. She had served her country well for a long career.

At the time Jamie went into the service, other women were getting married, but she chose a career not many women would have chosen. She very unselfishly served her country for 25 years with significant power and rank.

We all thank you Jamie.

✳ ✳ ✳

In retirement, Jamie continued to live in her Corte Madera home in Marin County, and according to her cousin David James, "She talks on the phone daily to her many friends." She had kept the house while she was overseas. But she had always wanted to have a cabin in the Wildwood. The cabin she built was at Bear Valley, in Calaveras County, in the mountains of California. They would have it for five and a half years. The cabin was contracted for as a livable shell. The entire family pitched in as a work party and did a lot of the finish work, painting it and putting in the tile squares for the floor covering. The colors of the living room and family room walls were painted in very vivid colors and you could see it through the windows from quite a ways away. The cabin had many bedrooms so all in the family could have their own room. There were multiple couches that could serve as beds also. Jamie and Bert had planned the cabin as a financial venture and to rent to vacationers and skiers.

The next summer, in 1969, after the cabin was built, the entire family went out on the train and spent Christmas at the Cabin in the Wildwood. Just before that first train trip, Esther's younger sister had died, so her older sister, Esther, and her Mom went on the trip. Her maternal grandmother was too ill to make the trip, but Bert and his wife Mavis went. John, their oldest stayed home to take care of Grandma. Esther's mother was now a widow and couldn't afford the trip and so Jamie paid for them. She would pay for many trips for them every few years at Christmas. Jamie wanted Esther and the rest of the family to know their Grandmother.

Jamie and her family had many happy family reunions there with her brother and his children and her mother. Her nephew David used to catch fish and they'd cook them for breakfast. Jamie loved the fresh air and smell of the pine trees and the view of the lake and she spent many happy hours on long walks to visit friends.

Unfortunately, the cabin burned down several years later.

In the summer of 1971, the town of Seymour, Iowa had their centennial and Jamie flew in to Kansas City and Esther went with her to the centennial. Uncle Bert and Mavis and Pam were there. They stayed with the family's good friend Dorothy Scott and Elsa Gump, who was one of their cousins.

Jamie's mother had done research on their family and this qualified Jamie for the DAR - the Daughters of the American Revolution. She was active in this group, as well as her niece Esther then living in close proximity to Jamie with her husband and daughter.

Jamie's Mother died in 1980. Jamie said to Bert, who was her brother and closest friend always, "I have got to get out of here. It upsets me too much to come home and she's no longer with me."

Jamie heard about new houses they were building at Rossmoor. One day Jamie climbed up a hill and saw the magnificent view from the highest hill in Rossmoor and the view was the most beautiful scene she had ever seen of the valley below and the majestic Mt. Diablo, so she went by the sales office and picked out a floor plan. This would be her home for over 25 years.

After retiring from the Army she had told her brother Bert she had to do something to make herself useful. She heard there was an opening for someone to inspect hospitals and nursing homes in the area. Jamie never really retired. She took the job and worked as surveyor for six years inspecting medical facilities. It was there she met her long time friend Dayton Shields who was a hospital administrator. Dayton organized Spite and Malice card games and a group gathered at Jamie's house daily to play, with prizes for winners. One of Jamie's loyal friends was Jean, her next-door neighbor. They played cards almost every night. Jean took Dayton home every night because he couldn't drive at this time in his life. Jean was a University of California at Berkeley professor who taught Adolescent Development courses. Another neighbor was Herschel Martin and his wife Ellen. Herschel fought at Monte Cassino in the Second World War and Jamie said to him, "You're a war hero." They had a little Shitzu dog called Poko who spent as much time with Jamie as with Herschel and Ellen.

Jamie has been honored for her educational, humanitarian and patriotic achievements. She has spoken before Veterans groups, State conventions, Service clubs, and DAR or Daughters of the American Revolution groups. She appeared on CBS Sixty Minutes, PBS, CNN, Nightline and the documentary No Time For Tears, also ABC's Good Morning America. Articles have been written about her in newspapers and she testified at the Senate Subcommittee hearings on Libraries and Memorials.

President Reagan signed legislation for the Vietnam Women's Memorial in 1988 as a symbol of the nation's gratitude to all US women who participated in the Vietnam conflict. The Senate voted 96 to 1 passing the bill for the memorial.

A proclamation from the White House honoring Jamie is dated March 29, 1991. It reads, "Because our Nation's greatness will be measured less by our wealth than by our willingness to help others. I am delighted to have learned of your generosity and hard work on behalf of your fellowman. You have earned the admiration of your colleagues and neighbors through your commitment to the values that have made our nation great. Duty, sacrifice and patriotism, that finds its expression in voluntary community service. Your efforts illustrate how each of us can make a difference in the lives of others, how each of us can be a shining Point of Light, in our community. I commend you for your achievements. Barbara joins me in wishing you continued success and every happiness, in the future. God Bless you. Sincerely, George Bush."

Because of Jamie's position as chairman of fund raising for the Vietnam Women's Memorial, she was presented before both the House and Senate in the California state capitol, where she was proclaimed by the 1991 California legislature Woman of the Year by Governor Willie Brown. She also was awarded the Woman of the Year for 1993 for Contra Costa County by California Congressman Bill Baker. Jamie was also Grand Marshal in a parade in Danville, California.

Jamie has many books on Vietnam, but she won't watch violent movies of any kind. She was asked to give speeches many times, and has certificates from the State of California, Letterman hospital in Tracy at the Army depot, where the Army supplies food to the troops. She has a certificate from the SAR or Sons of the American Revolution for contributing in war. She also has a certificate of the approval of the Vietnam Women's Memorial Project signed by former President George Bush Sr.

In the early 80's, Jamie also worked with Rose Sandecki, who is a very famous nurse and is the first woman Vietnam veteran to found a Vets Counseling Center in the country. The center was founded in 1981 in Concord, California. In those days it was exclusively for Vietnam veterans. At the time it was an outpatient center for veterans who didn't trust the Veterans Administration. The veterans would come and talk to other veterans about their problems.

Rose had four years of active duty in the Army including one year in Vietnam. She got out of the Army after two years service and then rejoined because she couldn't believe what she was hearing on the news about what was going on in Vietnam and all the protesting. She was going to make a career out of it but only stayed two years on active duty. She then joined an Army Reserve Medical unit. She retired in 1998 as a full bird Colonel from the Reserves. She also retired from the San Francisco VAMC in 2000.

Rose met Jamie when Jamie came into the Vets Center in Concord and they started talking. She asked Jamie if she would like to start volunteering at the center. Jamie was at the front desk greeting veterans and answering phone calls. She volunteered for several years. Rose praises Jamie for being so humble and so good with the veterans. She got very involved in veterans activities and veterans groups. It was important for her to do that kind of volunteer work.

Rose is mentioned in the first chapter of the book, A Piece of My Heart written by Keith Walker.

The Vets Center has a well-established program now and this Center is the leader in combat related Post Traumatic Stress Syndrome problems. Jamie worked with Denver Mills who is a Vietnam Veteran and who has been the Director of the Vets Center for the past 25 years.

CHAPTER 19

La Grande Dame

The Vietnam Women's Memorial

It took 10 years of her life and thousands of dollars to get the Vietnam Women's Memorial. Jamie said, "The memorial is my greatest accomplishment." Jamie is a National Treasure, and the Grande Dame of the Vietnam Women's Memorial.

Diane Carlson Evans, R.N., was an Army nurse who served in Vietnam from 1968-69, and the Founder and Chairman of the Vietnam Women's Memorial Foundation. She became the first woman in American history to spearhead a campaign to place a national monument in Washington, D.C. honoring military women. She served diligently, facing all odds to get the program on its feet. At the 10th anniversary of the founding of the memorial she recognized and honored Jamie as The Grand Dame of the memorial.

In October of 1983, Diane Carlson Evans started with the concept of a memorial to honor all military women and civilian women who had served during the Vietnam era. She held a meeting with the women and men interested in the project and started a non-profit corporation that conformed to IRS laws, developed a board of directors, abided by charities standards, set by-laws and developed information for articles of incorporation. Then, they had a press conference and publicized their mission.

In May of 1984, they officially got the papers of incorporation. This established the project as a non-profit 501(c) 3 corporation.

The Monument Project needed a sculpture so the corporation sponsored a design competition. But they needed to get approval of the Fine Arts Commission, the National Memorial Commission and they also needed President George Bush's approval. They had about 170 entries in the competition and they appointed judges to help them make a decision and finally decided on Glenna Goodacres' design of the three women nurses and a wounded man.

Jamie, who lived in California, had heard about the idea of the memorial in 1985 and sent Diane a letter. She talked about the wonderful girls who had been her nurses in Vietnam. She sent money and said she wanted to help out. Diane wasn't getting many letters from senior officers who said they wanted to help and this was the first Chief Nurse from the Vietnam War to contact her. Jamie said, "Just give me a job." Diane, in speaking about Jamie's nursing staff in Vietnam said, "They loved her because she rolled up her sleeves and worked with them. She did not sit in her office." Diane told Jamie they needed publicity and to speak at VFW, American Legion meetings and anywhere in California she could. Jamie got the word out. Once she started working on the project, she said she felt wonderful being back with the veterans.

Diane said, "Jamie is so kind and she commands respect. Jamie is very credible." Previously people wondered who Diane was and if she and her colleagues were going to abscond with the funds or were they really going to follow through. People were really reluctant to get involved or take a risk. Jamie did take a risk because she was a believer in all the goodness the memorial would command. Diane told Jamie about her husband Mike and her kids and where she grew up on a dairy farm in Minnesota. It was important to Jamie to have a friend from the Midwest. So they hit it off right away.

Jamie told Diane, "I'm with you to the very end with this." She worked on fund raising and publicity. She made contacts and made it her full time job.

"Jamie is so authentic and so sincere, who could turn her down?" Diane said. She told Jamie, "You are a hero. You were in three wars. You are an American heroine."

Jamie replied, "Diane, you're the first person who has told me that!"

Diane answered, "Well, that's pretty sad because the Chiefs of the Corps should have noticed and given you credit."

Diane and the Board of Directors did give her credit. They were constantly on the phone collaborating. Jamie became a good friend and she was also a mentor.

The Chief of the Corps or any of the other senior officers, didn't get behind the project until later because they simply weren't going to take the risk.

In 1986, Diane asked Jamie to serve on the Board of Directors. Jamie contributed tens of thousands of dollars and tens of thousands of hours to the memorial.

Jamie said to Diane, "You're the daughter I never had. Think of what we did because that's the best thing I ever did with my life."

Diane said, "She is not like a mother, but a dear friend." It's not only what she did for the memorial. It's what she did for Diane personally.

When Diane's integrity was under attack and her motives were challenged, she relied on Jamie to reaffirm the importance of the memorial and not be concerned about the agitators. There was a lot of mean spiritedness. Diane was called a radical feminist using the Vietnam dead to further her cause.

Diane, had four children under the age of 10, worked full time on the project and was getting tired of getting beat up. She told Jamie, "I'm getting too thin, I'm grinding my teeth at night, I'm losing my hair and my doctor tells me I have to get rid of the stress in my life. I just don't know if I can do this anymore." Jamie was the one who calmed her down and helped her get things in perspective.

Jamie was Diane's confidant along with her husband, but Jamie was an Army nurse and she really understood. Diane remembers calling her after getting a scathing letter from a retired high ranking member of the Nurse Corps. She told her her approach was all wrong, and she wasn't representing Army nursing the right way, and she was putting the Army's reputation at risk. Diane was devastated because this was not only a retired senior officer but also one from the Army Nurse Corps. Diane was looking for their help, not their enmity. She started wondering why she was doing all this.

When Diane told Jamie about this, Jamie's wise and calm wisdom helped her put things in their proper place. Jamie told her, "Forget about asking them for help, they won't get in there and do it, they will just tell you how to do it." Jamie never told Diane how to do anything. They made decisions together. Jamie would never talk down to anyone. She was a team player and would help solve problems rather than criticize. This was Jamie.

There was one point where there was dissension among the board members. It took Jamie, who was a neutral and respected person on the board to smooth things over, so they could move on and put aside these problems. It was good to have an older woman on the board. When Jamie spoke people listened to her out of respect because she was so ethical.

The effort to place the memorial in the nations capitol required two separate pieces of Congressional legislation and numerous hearings before the three federal commissions would approve it.

There was a very heated discussion about the placement of the statue and the site of the memorial at a hearing with the National Capitol Planning Commission. The commissioners targeted the design of the statue even though Diane, Glenna Goodacre and George Dickey had given their dissertations. They had reviewed all the charts and designs that were all very professional. It was very disturbing because it looked as if the project was going south again. The commission wanted to make changes, were going to send it back for more review and more staff discussions with their board, which would mean more delays. At this point Diane thought, "Here we go again, we make a few steps forward and several steps backward, and now this, after eight and a half years!"

Jamie was using a cane at this time and was sitting in the front row as usual. Her cane went down with a very loud thump and she said very loudly, "I'll be dead by then!" Jamie was very indignant. This must have made an impact and helped speed things along because it only took another six months after that to finalize everything. Then Glenna started sculpting the memorial.

✿ ✿ ✿

The Vietnam Women's Memorial Project was founded to promote healing of all women veterans from the Vietnam War, and others who served in Vietnam in humanitarian organizations and, through this memorial, to inspire future generations to serve their country in like manner. 250,000 served in Japan, Guam, Hawaii and the Philippines as well as Vietnam. It also was founded to identify these women and to educate the public. This memorial is a first in our country's history to honor women's patriotic service, and it also honors families who lost their loved ones who served. It stands next to the Vietnam Veteran's Memorial The Wall and the very impressive Frederick Hart Memorial of the three infantrymen in Washington, D.C. The Wall lists the names of 58,196 men and women who fought and died in Vietnam. The Vietnam Women's Memorial statue stands 6'8' tall and weighs one ton and honors the 11,000 women who served in Vietnam and the eight who died there. The memorial was designed by Glenna Goodacre.

Jamie said it was extremely difficult to raise funds for the memorial in the beginning because of the strong emotions spawned from the war, but she and others worked diligently to make the memorial a reality. They paid for their airline tickets and hotels and speaking expenses.

Jamie served as President of the Board of Directors for the memorial for one year, and as Treasurer, and was mainly in charge of the fund raising. When money was needed, she gave of her own savings so those needs would be met. One time she and Col. Jane Carson gave twelve thousand dollars each for books that needed to be published. Jane says "Our compensation was seeing the smiles on the soldiers faces." People were still not very receptive to anything to do with the Vietnam War.

Serving on the Board of Directors as well as serving as a fund raising Chairman was both fulfilling and challenging. She took her request for funding to the United States Congress, but her efforts failed. She gave speeches to local groups and worked tirelessly. The project would take years before the memorial became a reality.

One of the promotional posters for the memorial she had made was a picture of her dog tags and the poster for fund raising for the memorial that said, "Not all women wore love beads in the sixties."

The memorial was a life changing and healing instrument as much for the women as for the men. The women needed the recognition. They came home, went back to work, and just melded into society. It was years before it was recognized that the women had just as many psychological problems as the men.

Jamie spent many hours commuting between California and Washington, D.C. working on this project at her own expense. It took 18 years.

✡ ✡ ✡

Colonel Jane Carson was involved with the memorial from its inception. "Jamie was an inspiration to all of us. We always felt we were in the presence of a Duchess! I can't praise her enough because she is so unassuming." Jamie, when she was chief nurse in Vietnam, talked about her nurses as her kids. She was one of the few experienced nurses there and a wonderful teacher.

Jane graduated from Greenville in South Carolina. She served as a nurse in Chu Lai, Vietnam, which is 300 miles Northeast of Saigon, Ho Chi Minh City, in 1969 to 1970 at the 312th Evac Hospital. She was in one of the few Reserve units called up in the war.

Jane was a head nurse. She was evening supervisor and worked the ER and the medical ward in Vietnam. She got up at ungodly hours and staggered over to the ward, got a cup of coffee and worked twelve hours a day, six days a week. More was needed if push came to shove. They had a lot of malaria cases. The patients were in wracking pain and put on a platform, called the rack and put under a blanket. The men would say "Please don't put me on the rack." This was the only way to get the temperature down. The medicine they took made them as sick as the disease. In ER it was all drama and horrible. If a soldier got to the hospital quickly they had a 97% chance of surviving. In Vietnam they came out with more survivors because they were evaced out quickly and sent out to Japan or Hawaii. Most nurses cannot remember even one name of their patients. Blanking the names out is a survival mechanism. Some of the nurses don't want to talk about their experiences and that's too bad, because they are heroes in everybody's eyes.

There was a very tragic time when Sharon Lane was killed. She was Jane's staff nurse. Jane said, "I felt like I was so unprepared. I could never do enough."

"When Sharon was killed by in a rocket attack, she was the farthest away from the blast. Some Vietnamese patients were killed when shrapnel hit in the middle of the hospital. Sharon was killed by shrapnel. I was there just before it hit. They had just turned the lights on in the morning and I was getting ready to do reports and went down to talk to a corpsman at the end of the ward. When the rocket hit, the shrapnel went everywhere. We couldn't get to her quickly enough. I felt guilty somehow for not being able to help her but she died instantly. No one spoke about it and as head nurse, I just went on about my duty. We usually had three rocket attacks weekly.

"I wanted to bring back a Montanard baby. The Montanard s were the mountain people and were our allies in Vietnam. Little Mona was brought into the hospital by some adults. The entire village had been massacred by the Viet Cong. Jane claimed, "She wasn't much bigger than a grasshopper!" Mona had malaria and parasites. I couldn't leave her there. When I saw Mona I wanted to adopt her, but in those days a single woman could not adopt a child. My brother and sister-in-law adopted her. The good things you need to remember. Mona was a good thing that came out of the war."

✿ ✿ ✿

When the ground breaking for the memorial took place in 1992, Diane Carlson Evans and General and Chairman of the Joint Chiefs Colin Powell, Senator John Kerry from Massachusetts, Senator Paul Wellstone from Minnesota, Senator John Warner from Virginia, Glenna Goodacre and the entire board were present for ground breaking. Diane and Colin Powell shoveled the first shovel together.

✿ ✿ ✿

Glenna Goodacre was born in Lubbock, Texas, the second of two daughters. Glenna's art education consisted of attending Colorado College in Colorado Springs and Texas Tech in Lubbock, Texas. She later studied at the Art Students League in New York City. She is mother of two children, a son Tim who is a real estate broker, and Jill, a former Victoria's Secret model who is married to Harry Connick, Jr. Glenna started working as a portrait painter and then switched in 1969 to bronze sculptures.

When she saw Jamie at the dedication of the memorial in 1993, she said, "Jamie is the mother of them all. She is so respected and she treated everyone with equal honor. She doesn't realize what she has done, she is so humble."

The statue for the memorial was cast in bronze in Denver, Colorado by metalworker Jeanne Toussaint at Art Castings of Colorado. It was picked up there and taken by truck to Washington, D. C. by David Chung, a friend of the memorial and a Vietnam vet. He had a special truck made for the memorial with sides that rolled up and the Memorial was slid onto the truck. He drove through 22 cities and made stops at all these cities across the nation.

Col. Jane Carson accompanied the memorial statue from St. Louis into Washington, D.C. She says, "You are talking about a wonderful, wonderful experience. I saw women vets who would not even mention they were in the war and I saw them crying. Many of the men came up to thank us for what we had done to help them during the war. They were minus hands, or arms or legs, and you wondered if you had done them a favor."

✿ ✿ ✿

Dedication Day: November 11, 1993.

The day had finally arrived. A huge multitude of people gathered at the memorial. There were over 35,000 people from around the world as the memorial was dedicated. Hundreds of veterans placed flowers, cards, wreaths and service medals at the base of the memorial. There was much anticipation and excitement in the air as the US Air Force band played.

Jan Scruggs, President of the Vietnam Veterans Memorial Fund and founder of the Wall, opened the ceremony with a few words. "Ladies and gentlemen we are about to begin the ceremony and I am wondering if everyone is enjoying this beautiful day. I'd like to hear a round of applause for the US Air Force Band commanded by Chief Alan Fine. Everyone knows we are here today to thank the women who served alongside us during the Vietnam War. Besides the beautiful memorial, which is soon to be unveiled, and the warm feelings toward them, I thought it would be appropriate to show our thanks to the women who served during the Vietnam War." He began by honoring each branch of the service. The Army, Coast Guard, Navy, Marine Corps, US Air Force. "On behalf of the Vietnam Veterans Memorial Fund and the National Parks Service, I'm very pleased to welcome you to this historic day; my name is Jan Scruggs, I'll be Master of Ceremonies for just a little while. Today, history is being made, as we dedicate this very extraordinary work by Glenna Goodacre. Today represents many years of very dedicated work by Diane Evans and many others who have been associated with this project around the United States. They have given of themselves to honor the women who served our country bravely, as they have always done during time of war. From the Revolutionary War to currently in Somalia, women have served on active duty in the armed forces, and, also as civilians, they have always shown their patriotism and love of country. Today we recognize them. We will begin our ceremony with the posting of the colors.

"After the posting of colors I will introduce to you Diane Carlson Evans. Posting the colors today will be a joint services color guard of the military district of Washington; ladies and gentlemen, please stand for the posting of the colors."

After the guard marched around the draped memorial he continued, "We would now like to have a moment of silence for the infantry killed in Somalia a couple of weeks ago, may they rest in peace."

He continued, "The founder and chair of the Women's Vietnam Memorial has been working without pay or any breaks for 10 years to make this day a reality. For these past 10 years she has not been able to be with her family on Veterans Day. Coincidently, yesterday was her birthday. This is just about the first time she has been able to see her husband or her children all together in the same place at the same time on a veterans holiday. Her name is Diane Evans. She has sacrificed her time and her energy for a decade, so let's hear it for Diane and the other women who served alongside of her for the armed forces with the civilian women in Vietnam. Sacrifice is nothing new. The sacrifice she has put in for the past 10 years to make this memorial a reality is nothing new. Many in the audience were like me, wounded, and were attended to by nurses and other American women who answered their country's call to duty. Diane served with the United States Army Nurse Corps in Pleiku and Bung Tao in Vietnam. Probably some of you here today were helped by Diane Evans. If not by Diane, if you were wounded in Vietnam, I can guarantee you the nurse who served you and helped bandage your wounds is in this audience, because just about every woman who served in Vietnam is here today. Some were nurses, some were Red Cross workers, some were with the Department of State, or with civilian agencies, but they all need to be thanked, and today they are being thanked. Diane symbolizes compassion and patriotism. She exemplifies the qualities of all the women who served over there. Ladies and gentlemen, I now turn over the program to Diane Carlson Evans." There was a huge round of applause.

Diane Carlson Evans who was master of ceremonies spoke. "Today is truly a day of the people, by the people, and for the people and the sun is shining on us. Children, ladies and gentlemen, please join Senior Master Sergeant Julie Turentine, United States Air Force, as we sing the National Anthem."

After the National Anthem, Diane introduced Rev. Alice Farquhar-Mayes who was a nurse in Vietnam from 1967 to 1968. She later flew Medivac missions as a flight nurse out of Tan son Nhut, Cam Ranh Bay, and Da Nang from 1969 to 1971. Alice went on to earn a Master of Divinity degree and served as Chaplain at St. Luke's Regional Medical Center in Boise, Idaho, for 13 years where she made good use of her training as nurse and priest. She also served as a parish priest for many years. She retired in 2009.

Chaplain Farquhar-Mayes began.

"Let us begin with a moment of silence;

A moment to let ourselves to be truly present to this place,

to this time, to one another and to God...

O God of light and God of darkness, God of all Creation.

We dare to claim - and proclaim - Your presence here among us.

We dare to claim this as Holy Ground - holy because YOU are here;
     holy because WE are here.
We seek your blessing on what we do here this day,
and on each one of us, however we have come:
… in body … spirit … prayer;
… in person or through modern technology.

We give you thanks as this day has finally come, We have waited long, worked hard, prayed often and sometimes despaired. We give you thanks for all who have supported us and loved us along the way, and for those who have gone before us on the journey home. O Timeless God of all our days and years, surround us with your love.

We who waited and worked and worried were forever changed;
We who went willingly into the hell to bring hope, heart, healing, humanity, came home forever changed;
We who went into the hell armed with compassion, knowledge, smiles, and tears came home forever changed;
We who went into the hell with the willingness to touch, to hold, to listen, to care came home forever changed.

We were - and are - Everywoman.

We now come to you at this sacred time
… to remember … and to be remembered;
We come to bear witness … and to be heard;
… to honor … and to be honored;
… to touch … and to be touched;
… to celebrate … and to Come Home.
We come to heal … and to be healed;
We come so that our pain may be assuaged … and our joy made full.

We come, perhaps most of all, to pray for PEACE, to declare without equivocation that all war is appalling and abhorrent - to you and each of us here gathered.

O God, who redeems the past and to make all things new,
Come to us and be in us this day, make us ready for what we are about to begin.
Be light to our darkness, and peace to our pain.

Give us, both solace and strength, pardon and renewal.
Then we shall find the way of laughter - and the victory will go to Love.
Amen."

It's a Grand Old Flag was played, and then Diane said, "Welcome my sister veterans of the Vietnam War, my fellow veterans, and all veterans of all wars. Welcome Secretary of Veterans Affairs Jessie Brown and other distinguished members of the administration, Congress, of whom we have many members here today, also from the Senate and House of Representatives. Welcome members of our armed forces.

"A very special welcome to our new Chairman of the Joint Chiefs of Staff, General John M. Shalikashvili. The General will honor all Vietnam era military women veterans at a special joint forces parade tomorrow at 11:00 AM at ceremonial hall at Ft. Myer, Virginia. He is inviting all of you who served during the Vietnam War and the United States military to join him. He is going to welcome us home to the United States of America for the first time in a military ceremony. Thank you to the National Park Service and the General Services Administration, which has helped to make this day possible. Welcome Jan Scruggs, and the Vietnam Women's Memorial Project Board of Directors, welcome friends of our Territories and Canada, Australia, New Zealand, Korea, Vietnam, and all those who have come here from many parts of the world today to be with us who are veterans and friends. Welcome everyone. Today has been a long time coming. It is a day that we have long, long waited for. We have started this morning with the celebration march where we joined together. We are here to dedicate this memorial. And this evening at 7 o'clock PM, we will have a candlelight ceremony where we can come together again here at this monument. There is a special group of people here with us today who, without their organization's belief in the vision to place this memorial to women on this site, we would not be dedicating this memorial. Without their backing, their work, we would not be dedicating this memorial. Would the Veterans Service Organization National leaders representing millions of our nations veterans please stand or wave and give a proud salute as I introduce you: The National Commander of the American Legion of America, Vietnam veteran Bruce Theison, National Junior Vice Commander of the Veterans of Foreign Wars, Vietnam veteran Paul Spira standing in for National Commander George Cramer, Junior Vice Commander of the Disabled American Veterans, Gregory Reed, President of the Vietnam Veterans of America, Vietnam veteran James Brazie, President of the Paralyzed Veterans of America, Vietnam veteran

Richard Johnson. We thank them. We thank all who have brought the gift of hope, this gift of healing. Representing the thousands of families who lost loved ones of the Vietnam war please stand: President of Gold Star mothers, Jean Penrod, and the President of the Gold Star Wives, Paula Moot. To our Native Americans brother and sister veterans, who walked across the country and who stood watch at this monument during this past weekend today, thank you. Today we are one people, united we stand, strong and proud."

"The Vietnam Women's Memorial Project's Board of Directors: Diane Carlson Evans, Doris Lippman, Evangeline Jamison, Jane Carson, Shirley Crowe, Judy Heline, Dan Daly, Willy Blakeman, Executive Director Diana Hellinger, plus Sculptor Glenna Goodacre, Landscape Architect George Dickey, and Robert Stanton of the National Park Service will now unveil the Vietnam Women's Memorial."

The Vietnam Women's Memorial was draped with a red, white and blue parachute. While beautiful, soft music played, the Board, and sculptor Glenna Goodacre formed a semi-circle around the memorial and together they all unveiled the statue.

When the memorial was unveiled, tears flowed everywhere. Everyone was in awe of the beauty of the memorial. After some poignant moments with beautiful music playing, there were a few moments of silence. As the Board members for the memorial started to walk back to their seats, Jamie blew a kiss to everyone on the platform. The memorial stands on the grounds of the Vietnam Veterans Memorial in Washington D.C., 300 feet southeast of the statue of three servicemen near the Vietnam Veterans Wall of Names.

After the memorial was unveiled, Diane Carlson Evans said, "We have just unveiled the first monument in the history of the United States dedicated at our nation's capital honoring the military women who served during war time. Welcome home, daughters of America, welcome home my sister veterans. Allow the love and the pride that fills this hallowed space tender in your hearts and souls forever as we continue on our journey in life. During the years 1966 to 1972 I considered it a great privilege to be entrusted to care for the wounded soldiers of the Vietnam War, and it has been an equally great privilege and honor to spend the past 10 years, albeit 10 long difficult years, to work with you, so many of you here today. It is for you a dream, to honor you my sister veterans and all of you who served in the Vietnam era that we stand here on sacred ground at our nations capital to finally say thank you. Today for the first time in more than 20 years since we returned home from the war, we are here together again.

We are also here for the families who lost loved ones during that war, and for the MIAs and POWs. To my sister veterans, "How does this make you feel today, to know how tirelessly your brother veterans worked to help make this day possible for you? To my brother veterans, how proud we were to serve with you and now to stand with you in bronze on this site forever. How many of the more than 265,000 military and civilian women who volunteered to serve throughout the world during that period of time are here today?

"You were all supposed to receive for the women who served in the military a red, white and blue arm band and women wearing a solid blue arm band was to designate the civilian veterans. For those of you who are wearing them and for those of you who see them wearing them, please give them a big hug. Other women veterans raise your hand so we know where you are. At this time I would like to ask everyone to look around and turn to these women and please say, Welcome home and thank you for what you did. Let no one ever again mistake - who you are. Let no one ever forget you again and what you did for this nation and don't ever hide the fact again that you are a veteran of the Vietnam War. It's been a long journey here from Vietnam and other parts of the world where you served. But the journey for most of us still isn't over. Many of us are just beginning their healing but this is our place to start. We have waited for this day but we have also feared for this day. We feared that it would never happen. We feared that the nation wouldn't care. We feared that we would never find a monument that would meet the approval of a federal agency of this town. We feared that those who said ours was an impossible dream were maybe right and some of us veterans even feared to come to this wall and I know that there are women who have come today to the wall for the very first time. Today we need to set those fears aside because veterans have prevailed in their determination about what is right and what is good about the nation and for one another and we come together in love and we celebrate the patriotism and courage of Vietnam veterans and all veterans. The right thing has happened and the right people came along to make it happen and some of them are our speakers today.

"We have worked with many wonderful people in the National Park Service who have helped make this day possible. We are very pleased to have with us today Robert Stanton, the Regional Director of the National Capitol region of the National Parks Service to share his remarks about the placement of this monument on federal grounds where it will be entrusted to the Park Service forever. As Regional Director he is responsible for some 40 national parks, monuments, and a memorial in a region, which attracts more than 40 million visitors annually. Please welcome a true friend to the Vietnam Women's Memorial and the Vietnam Women's Memorial Project - Robert Stanton."

Robert Stanton thanked Diane not only for her decision to allocate such a memorial to the women who served in the Vietnam war but to extend that friendship with the National Park Service and the Department of the Interior to ensure the preservation of this memorial would always be here to remind the American people of the contribution so many women and men made to the Vietnam war. He thanked Jan Scruggs, the founder of the Vietnam Veterans Memorial reconfirming their partnership with them and his commitment in partnership in the future. He talked about how the memorial was built on the spirit of volunteerism. He selected a volunteer, Ms. Bobbie Keith, to lay a wreath at the memorial on behalf of the National Parks Service. He quoted President Lincoln: "There are those who gave their full measure of devotion, their lives, for this country and for their love of God." He concluded that, "For those of us at the National Parks Service it is an honor and privilege. So when you return here each year, you will find the memorial maintained in the very best of order." A very appreciative audience applauded.

✿ ✿ ✿

Diane introduced Harry G. Robinson. She said, "It is my great pleasure to introduce Harry G. Robinson. Harry served in Vietnam from 1966 to 1968 as a Ranger Qualified Combat Unit Commander. He served with the 1st Infantry Division assigned to company D, First-Engineer Batallion. Harry was awarded the Bronze Star, and the Purple Heart. He was medivaced to Long Binh where under his watch was a grey haired military woman who had already served more than 20 years beginning with WWII and Korea. Along the medical evacuation chain from South East Asia to Walter Reed Army hospital were the many women who served to get him home alive. He currently serves as Dean and Professor of Urban Design at the School of Architecture and Planning at Howard University. Please welcome Harry Robinson, a Vietnam veteran."

Harry, after being introduced, waved at Jamie and said, "Hi Jamie!" Then he continued, "Platform guests, friends, my former comrades in arms and first and last today, the woman who brought our Nation to this high moment and who proved that true heroism is enduring one more moment, the heroes' hero, Diane Carlson Evans. Today the indelible connections that bind us together as one people have been forged in a small, yet significant way. Today we are united through form and spirit in this special place of moral authority and strength of mind. This place, which speaks in thunderous silence, through and with the voices and hearts of many.

"The language of this statue symbolizing our comrades resonates the message of moral obligation, spiritual imperative and historic trust, its moral obligation is to be, at once, both physical and transparent and to communicate their courage, endurance, grief, horror and rage. Yet, their sacred commitment to mission, duty, honor, and country, their central roles in the Vietnam War and their sacrifices of spirit, soul, humanity, their very being, and the ultimate sacrifice their lives were accepted as within their responsibilities. Their moral obligation reminds the thousands of us whose pain they shared, and whose bodies and minds that they cared for, and whose hearts that they uplifted, that their roles of maintaining dignity where none existed as the weight of war pressed all within its grasp, and extinguished hope where only hopelessness prevailed.

"There, for a brief period, they were our mothers and sisters and eternally our comrades, our friends. They were part of a network of more than 65,000 women in the armed forces throughout the world, including not only those in country but equally women supporting the war on training bases, medical centers, command centers, air-wings, and on ships. That in their strength they challenged the mind of death with their love of life and to their challenge of anguish, cast their ability to hope and mask the darkness of their despair and matching it with the treasures of their dreams. Such is the moral obligation of this monument.

"The spiritual imperative of this statue dedicated here today defies the narrow, symmetrical, critical reviews of mere mortals. It concedes nothing to its critics and it expects nothing from them. Some things are beyond criticism, mystical even.

"To engage the value of this statue one must understand what our native American comrades call The Vision Quest of Diane Evans and her magnificent effort with Lippman, Jamison, Carson, and many others equaling that of King, Randolph, Abernathy and Wilkins as they planned to March on Washington.

"We must also understand closure and that mystical power works in circles. In the words of Robert Kincade, analysis destroys wholes, some-things. Many things are meant to stay whole. If you look at the pieces they go away. The power of the big idea of this great memorial is larger than, higher than, wider than, deeper than our most profound consciousness. It has second sight, the ability to see into the future and complete the circle of life at the Wall. In turn, the Wall embraces the statue and adds dimension to its meaning. The statue is inclusive of all in its gentle understanding. It is, at peace and one with the threshold between the here and the hereafter. At rest on this site, it exerts neither dominance, nor ego. It is as were the women in our armed forces during our war, non-political, and pure in its presence and in its intensions. It represents and honors all that is good and right about our great nation. It represents an honor for each and all of us. Here in this statue, the historic trust of the women of our country's military efforts is preserved. The Vietnam era women will continue the heritage of Margaret Corbin, Debra Sampson Ginnett, Mary Mother Picodite, Clara Barton, Harriet Tubman, Suzie King Taylor, and Sally Thompkins. All of whom in the words of James Baldwin, paid for with the contemporary excellence of our women in this country's armed forces. In the silence of simply being this monument cultivates time and authenticity within the solitude of our inner selves. It is a container of hope and is the truth between time and eternity. It has recreated the bonds between and the family of our veterans. It has stopped becoming. It is full testimony to the history of the contributions of each and every woman. Thank you." A thunderous applause followed his speech.

Diane spoke: "Our goal for adding a memorial here, as you know, took years, years of effort of volunteers and staff, it took money, but there is only one person who's understanding heart and gifted hands created the monument before you. Because of this woman we have unveiled a bronze Monument which shall stand forever. Glenna Goodacres' sculpture portraying American women and a wounded male soldier honors the living, those who came home from the Vietnam War. This will be a reminder of our daughters and sons and all future generations that America is strong because of men and women supporting each other by working and serving together. After 40 years of achievement, Glenna Goodacre is frequently challenged to defend her artistic perspective. Public art is controversial turf. How well we know, but Glenna Goodacre of Santa Fe, New Mexico, does not need to explain or defend her work of art to us because we understand and we don't care what the art critics say. We did not build this memorial for the critics and they do not need to come here to critique it. One day while watching Glenna work on the clay form of a figure in her studio in Santa Fe, New Mexico, she told me to take a chunk of clay and hold it. She went about her work and I realized what I was holding. I was holding clay from the earth. She took this enormous amount of earth and turned it into what you see before you - a portrayal of the best America has to offer - her young men and women. At this time I would like to thank her. Thank Glenna Goodacre, as she stands before you to share in this story."

After a standing ovation, Glenna shared her thoughts: "What a day! Distinguished guests, my family, and friends. My design to create a lasting tribute to the women who served in Vietnam is founded upon my deep respect for each and every one of them. My initial research gave me the ideas for the composition and then for three years of perfecting the design, I came to know these women and I heard their stories. With my clay, I wanted to reflect their emotions - their courage, compassion, and their dedication. The woman who is holding the soldier I've always called the nurse. You know 90 percent of the women who served in Vietnam were nurses. She's holding this soldier. She cradles him across her lap. She is seated on the ever-present sandbags. When I was researching, every picture I looked at of Vietnam, there were sandbags. So this being a moment of crisis in time it seemed natural for me, she wanted to help him, she needed to elevate him, and she needed to sit down on the sandbags and pull him up in her lap. To me this man is unconscious, but he will live. I purposely covered the top of his face so he would become more anonymous, so he could be anyone's son, he could be a brother, or he could be a father. She is serving as his last support. The standing woman is looking up perhaps for the Medivac helicopters. Maybe she is looking up for help from God. She has her hand on the nurses' elbow. Diane has told me that so many of the nurses read so much into that because it shows the compassion, the feelings they had for each other, because they became such close friends during the time they served. Both her hands and her face express her anxiety in this moment of crisis. The kneeling woman has been called by so many of the veterans as the heart and soul of the piece. As I was working on this in Santa Fe, a group of veterans came in and visited and they would watch the development of the piece, and they would say, "That was me, that was how I felt." She's staring at an empty helmet and this epitomized the agony of the war, the despair, and the frustrations that so many of the veterans felt. Nothing is complete, in that the edges are fuzzy purposely so that you can finish this yourself. There are no regiment-patches, and there are no bars, no definition of rank. I did this on purpose so you could place yourself into this piece, you could put yourself anywhere in Vietnam and feel a part of this.

"From my original sketches to this resulting bronze sculpture, this has been a phenomenally rewarding experience. I am humbled by the overwhelming gratitude of the veterans, the tears, and the many thank yous will last me a lifetime. That my hands can shape the clay, which might touch the hearts and heal the wounds of those who served, fills me with deep satisfaction. But it is Diane Evans that deserves all our gratitude. If it weren't for her, we wouldn't be here." Glenna looked at Diane and said, "Isn't that right?"

"She is the most tenacious, most determined, ferocious single-minded woman I have ever known. Her family has given her up for 10 years. My son Eric told me the other day Mom used to make bread every day, but they've had to buy a bread maker. I'm proud of my sculpture. I hope you are too. Diane, here it is, veterans this is for you. After the ovation for Glenna, Diane said; "Every project has its champion. Those individuals who stand up for the cause saying, 'Now, what can I do to help?' then giving and asking for nothing in return but to see us working hard and giving it our best effort. It is with great honor and respect that I introduce to you one of these people, Admiral William J. Crowe. You might say that this Navy man was hooked, first when he met and married Shirley, second from the moment he learned about the Vietnam Women's Memorial project's first major blow, our 1987 first official rejection for this site. His comment then and his no nonsense tone was, 'What's the problem here?' At that time he was serving his second term as the 11th Chairman of the Joint Chiefs of Staff. His distinguished career following graduation from the U.S. Naval Academy in 1946 includes sea tours with submarines, senior advisor to the Vietnamese Riverine force, Republic of Vietnam, and numerous positions that put him in command around the world from Europe to the Persian Gulf. Please welcome this very special American patriot and friend to us, the soldier, the sailor, the airman and the veteran called Admiral William J. Crowe retired, United States Navy."

Admiral William J. Crowe USN (Ret.) began, "What a joyful and emotional occasion. I can't tell you what a pleasure it is to participate in a ceremony where it's not only proper, but, appropriate to express your emotions, nostalgia, humanity, and if you want to cry, and there's a lot of crying going on today. I hear of this New World Order a lot. I don't know if we've got a new world order or not but we have a new domestic order, I can assure you of that and if anyone doesn't believe that, they can stand where I am and can see this sea of happy, celebrating women they would know today in Washington has been overwhelmed by women and that's not all bad. As a matter of fact, that's the way it should be. On this Veteran's Day, which is incidentally the 75th anniversary of the conclusion of the armistice of World War I, our nation is finally getting a chance to complete the circle to say thank you to those women who wore the uniform in the Vietnam War and especially those who actually served in country during that conflict. I can't tell you how honored I am to participate in this ceremony. For the last several years I have had the privilege of watching at close hand as Diane Carlson Evans and her faithful lieutenants have struggled with the Washington bureaucracy - oh my goodness it was a titanic struggle, and they won. I enjoyed my association but I must be frank with you. It partly sprang from the fact that my wife is on the board. I must tell you never underestimate the power of nagging. But I have enjoyed every moment of it and I have appreciated and I have admired these women. They have now knocked over all the windmills and slain all the dragons that stood in the way. They deserve our heartfelt gratitude for their performance above and beyond the call of duty.

"The lovely bronze that we dedicate today stands not only as a reminder of a painful era, it was a painful era, we all went through it, but more importantly, as a tribute to an exceptional group of American women who answered their country's call at an extraordinary time in our history and did so at great personal sacrifice. This touching piece memorializes the nurses, Red Cross workers, those of you in USO units, intelligence specialists, photographers, air-traffic controllers, the whole spectrum of female volunteers. And I think you would all agree that Glenna Goodacre's artistry has captured the spirit, the passion and the dedication of these unusual women in a most sensitive fashion and the previous speaker was most eloquent in describing that. No one can better testify to the appropriateness of this memorial than the men who served in Vietnam and this audience is full of them.

"I'm going to presume on your patience for a moment to repeat a vivid memory of my own. I was standing in an open space late at night watching a Medivac helicopter threading its way through trees, telephone poles, and guy wires to a landing just outside of Ca Mau, one of the metropolises at the foot of the delta. I was with six US Marines and Sailors who rushed into burning huts just after a Vietcong attack and rescued eight small Vietnamese children. Although it was against the rules and after some spirited dialogue, we persuaded the nearest US hospital in Bien Tuy to accept these children. Of course it was 80 miles away. Each of us was holding in our arms a severely burned child. But as that helicopter settled on the ground and a young Army nurse jumped out, she took complete charge. With skill and kindness, she administered first aid, she arranged the children in the helicopter with loving care and she comforted the assembled parents. There was only room for one escort, so she presided over a meeting to help the parents select which adult would accompany the children to the hospital. As the helicopter lifted off and faded into the darkness, I couldn't help thinking, I have just seen an angel of the Lord at work. What I am trying to say is make no mistake, this monument celebrating the achievement of women is as extremely important to men as well, especially to Vietnam veterans. Your contributions were vital and are deeply appreciated by those of us who were nurtured by your professionalism and compassion. Truly, the nation is indebted to the women being honored today. We could never fully repay that debt but this statue acknowledges in a modest way that obligation for all of us.

"I have only one more thought. Perhaps the most enduring aspect of this memorial will not be the remembrances or memories that it evokes, but the impact it has on the future. It says something profound about what courageous and determined individuals can do. What a marvelous example it represents. A role model so to speak. What a marvelous example it will be for the coming generations of young American women. Hopefully, it will inspire them to dream, to strive, to challenge adversity and not to be intimidated by peril. What a wonderful legacy for the women who served during Vietnam to leave to this country." There was a standing ovation.

Diane introduced General George Price who read a speech written by Diane.

Vice President Al Gore spoke.

✿ ✿ ✿

Diane introduced Francis Whitebird. "We have a very, very special person with us at this time who's going to do something special with and for all of us. Francis Whitebird is a member of the Lakota nations of South Dakota. Francis served two tours in Vietnam, first in the 196th Light Infantry Brigade and then with the 95th Evac hospital in Da Nang. (People cheer) You're a popular guy! He comes from a long line of Native American patriots and is very proud of his father who served in Europe in World War II as a Lakota Code Talker. Francis will now ask for participation in a Centering Ceremony."

Francis says, "We all need to do this together, so would you please stand up. You have to face west. We will go counter-clockwise. We pray to the grandfather who sits where the sun goes down and paints his face black. We call to the thunder-beams who nourish the world. We ask

148

for nourishment of healings for our minds and our bodies. Turn to the north. We pray to the grandfather who sits where the wintery ice is. As the buffalo nation, we ask the spirit of the buffalo as he faced the storm, we ask those people who support God and country, for without these values we would not be free. Face to the east. We pray to the direction where the sun comes up and we ask for our patience for new life and we ask our sister the Morning Star so that we may be strong and so that we can protect our country and that new people will follow our lead. Turn to the south. We pray to the direction where the summer resides. May grandfather, who paints his face yellow and the spirit world give us help, help with our minds and our bodies. We pray to the clouds. We pray to the grandfather who resides where the clouds reside and paints his face blue. We ask the eagles and as we call them now, we ask them so they can guide us as they can see. (He blows a whistle). We pray to the grandmother earth, grandmother earth gives us everything and takes everything away. We thank grandmother for the red day. Red is the color of blood of all of our relatives and our brothers and sisters, the animals. Red is in the color of our flag, red is the color of the dawn of the new day and also red is the color in the rainbow. As we center ourselves, we pray to all the grandfathers and the grandmothers and as we are here, the center of our environment is our body and through our body is our heart. In our heart we ask that we have love for each other, we have respect and courage. Be generous with our material goods and also our time. We ask these so that we can all live in a full circle of life and be in harmony with all our relatives." (He blows whistle to end the speech). Loud Applause.

✳ ✳ ✳

Diane introduced the next person. "We are pleased and honored today to have with us a young American who is proud to be an American who through his music wishes to extend gratitude to the nation's women veterans during this celebration of patriotism and courage. Harry Connick Jr."

After Harry Connick Jr. sang America, Diane introduced Colonel Amelia Jane Carson. "Our keynote speaker today is Colonel Amelia Jane Carson, United States Army Nurse Corps retired. Colonel Carson, Jane to us who know her and love her, was raised in South Carolina. She entered the Army as a second Lieutenant in 1962 during the Cuban Missile Crisis.

She remained in the Army Nurse Corps for 27 years. Colonel Carson's assignments included two tours in Korea and one year in Vietnam assigned to the 312th Evacuation hospital and the 91st Evacuation hospital in Chu Lai from 1969 to 1970. Her distinguished career included duty at the Pentagon as Chief Nurse for the National Guard. In 1984, a veteran from Wisconsin, upon hearing about the project, told me to call Colonel Carson. She told me, 'She'd want to support this effort.' Jane has been a supporter and volunteer, from that time. Her military qualities of duty, leadership and commitment immediately transferred to the Vietnam Women's Memorial Project upon her retirement in 1990. Among her responsibilities for the Project was that of supervising and working closely with our national corps of volunteers. Before I ask Jane to come forward, would all of the regional and state corps of volunteers of the Vietnam Memorial Project please rise so that we may thank you with a grateful round of applause. Colonel Jane Carson."

Colonel Jane Carson spoke: "Thank you very much Diane, my dear, dear friend. My friend Al Gore, distinguished guests, family and friends and honored, Sister and Brother Veterans.

"It is an incredible honor for me to speak to you at this historic event. I'm sure a lot of my friends were having doubts because every year I kept telling them, Next year we will dedicate the memorial! And next year never came because we had an unexpected setback.

"Well, thanks to the inspiration, dedication and perseverance of this lady, Diane Carlson Evans, who kept the dream alive even in the darkest hours and a lot of work from our staff, faithful volunteers and supporters, we are here at long last to dedicate this beautiful sculpture by Glenna Goodacre.

"Just as the Wall memorializes the men and women who made the ultimate sacrifice for our country and the statue of the three service men welcomes home our brother veterans who made it back to the world, now the Vietnam Women's Memorial will Welcome Home our Sister Veterans and complete the circle of healing. To quote Diane, "We are dedicating...a beautiful monument that portrays all that is good about the service, all that is tragic and horrible about war, and an everlasting statue that begs for peace. From this day forward, it will be a place of healing and hope for thousands of women veterans who suffer invisible and silent wounds of war. It will stand as a symbol for all generations of the enduring legacies of strength, courage, compassion and caring portrayed by the military and civilian women who faithfully served at home and abroad during a very difficult time for our nation. Regardless of occupation or location, each person's job was just as important as the others. We were not drafted into the military. We volunteered to serve in time of need, like women have done since the founding of this nation.

"I joined the Army Nurse Corps in 1962 during the Cuban Missile Crisis. A few years later, like most women who went to Vietnam, I volunteered. Our soldiers were being sent there so that's where I felt a compelling need to be.

"Most of us were in our early to mid 20's and very idealistic. The soldiers we treated were also very young - the average age being 19 years old. Very few of us knew what to expect in the guerilla warfare.

"In April 1969, I arrived at the 312th Evacuation Hospital in Chu Lai, located about 300 miles north of Saigon on the beautiful South China Sea. On my first night in Chu Lai, I was sitting on the patio of the Officer's Club watching what I thought at the time was a beautiful display of fire flashes. Someone mentioned that it was a firefight. The next day the reality of what that meant hit home when I saw the results of that fire- fight the next day. Needless to say, the display of fire flashes were never considered beautiful to me again.

"While experience varied based on where we were assigned, many saw the results of war every day.

"We took care of patients who were savagely mutilated by high velocity weapons, rockets, booby traps and land mines. Even if we were able to save a soldier's life, we wondered how he or she would ever be able to deal with the emotional wounds. Medical diseases, such as malaria and dengue fever that racked the body with pain, had to be contended with.

"There were no front lines or safe rear areas. Because of guerilla tactics, many military and civilian women were in the middle of conflict. At Chu Lai, rocket attacks and snipers were common. Early one morning in June of 1969, a rocket hit a hospital ward and killed one of my dedicated staff nurses, Lt. Sharon Ann Lane. It was always hard to lose the life of any of our soldiers – to be unable to save a friend and colleague wounded in the middle of the hospital compound was devastating. Until recently, I have blocked that from my memory because it was too painful to deal with.

"Many of us came home with a lot of guilt and shame for not being able to do more – for not being able to save more lives – for sometimes being afraid that we would not measure up. Instead of dealing with the painful feelings and memories, we buried them deep inside.

"I met Sharon Lane's mother, Mrs. Kay Lane, for the first time last night. To be able to hug her was like hugging Sharon and saying, Welcome

Home. Sharon's name is etched on the wall along with the other seven other military women who died. They are: Eleanor Grace Alexander, Pamela Dorothy Donovan, Carol Ann Drazba, Annie Ruth Graham, Elizabeth Ann Jones, Mary Therese Klinker, Hedwig Diane Orlowski.

"We are honored to have with us today families of many of the military and civilian women who made the ultimate sacrifice for their country.

"We returned to a country in turmoil that did not understand and did not even want to hear what we had just experienced. The country wanted to forget Vietnam and, as a consequence, the men and women veterans who had done their best for their country were not only forgotten, but were sometimes treated with disdain and dishonor. This young nurse who proudly went off to Vietnam found it hard to understand why my Army green uniform was the target of cruel jokes and sometimes, outright hostility.

"Of the many thousands of military and civilian women who served during the Vietnam War, we have only located 11,500. Just as the Wall provided the catalyst for our brother veterans to start healing, many women veterans have started the healing journey as a direct result of the Vietnam Women's Memorial. Diane was personally responsible for starting me and countless others on the road to healing.

"Yet, a lot of women still have not yet shared their personal stories with others and some cannot even admit that they are Vietnam veterans. The pain is too deep and has been packed away too long. I am reminded of the women who came to tears when they saw the statue on the whistle stop tour. Many admitted that they had never told anyone that they were Vietnam veterans. It was an honor to thank them and welcome them home. So many said to thank Diane and all the people who made this possible – they had not realized how much they needed this monument.

"I was afraid that my heart would break if I ever allowed any of my emotions to surface, but as Alice Walker states in her book "The Temple of My Familiar", sometimes... Breaking the heart - opens it.

"We must be able to break the heart to remember the pain and let go so that we can move on. 'Forgiving is not forgetting - forgiving is remembering and letting go,' said Claudia Black.

"If we are to heal, forgiveness is a must, no matter how hurt or betrayed we feel – and self forgiveness is the start of our healing journey so that we can forgive others.

"We know the price that our fallen brothers and sisters on the wall made.

"We know the sacrifice that their families and friends made.

"Let us, as women veterans, not forget the price that we each paid for serving our country during the Vietnam War, and surviving that war.

"Let us remember, forgive, and let go, so that we can get on with the fullness of life.

"Let us be aware of each other's pain and provide the needed support to encourage healing.

"Love, forgiveness, and healing are what this beautiful memorial is all about.

"In tribute to our brothers and sisters whose names are etched on the Wall, let us come together in love, peace, and forgiveness to support each other as we all, Come Home. Welcome home my friends."

A thunderous applause followed her speech.

Secretary of the Veterans Affairs Jesse Brown spoke next: "Ladies and Gentlemen, to honor the Vietnam era women veterans, wreaths will now be placed by the following organizations." After all the many veterans' groups and those associated with the memorial laid their wreaths he continued, "Representing the Vietnam Memorial Project are Diane Carlson Evans, Jane Carson, Evangeline Jamison, Doris Lippman, accompanied by Vice President Al Gore." Together they placed the wreath at the memorial.

Taps was played and the benediction, was said by Rev. Alice Farquhar.

Jan Scruggs said, "Please remain standing while Crystal Gayle sings the official theme song for the dedication of the Vietnam Women's Memorial, 'Til the White Dove Flies Alone written for this day by the composers Rod McBrian, and John Lund."

"Ladies and Gentlemen, those of you who have seats please be seated. At this time the board members of the Vietnam Women's Memorial Project will be joined by Vice President Al Gore as they follow the National Park Police Honor Guard for the laying of the wreath at the Vietnam Veterans Memorial. Joining them will be the Vietnam Veterans Memorial Fund two of our volunteers will be laying a wreath at the memorial. Please remain in place as Diane Carlson Evans, Jane Carson, Evangeline Jamison, and Doris Lippman accompany the Vice President." Patriotic music was played as they laid the wreath at the memorial.

✪ ✪ ✪

All these women achieved something that amounted to Monumental Proportions in building this monument. It portrayed the great compassion and dedication of the women who served. They have been committed to building on that foundation, committed to furthering the education and research and also identifying the women who served. The memorial stands for the gallant ladies who had courage in the face of fear and the unknown. It stands for healing of all wounds of those who served. It stands for all to see what women in the service for their country have done in this the longest of all of our wars, the Vietnam War. The monument is a testament for all of these things.

CHAPTER 20

Memorial Debt Retirement

The Vietnam Women's Memorial Project still had a large unpaid debt but the Board of Directors had not given up and hoped to be able to retire the debt quickly. The VWMP still needed to raise one million dollars to pay off the design, construction, landscaping and maintenance for the memorial and the dedication ceremonies.

Late one night, Diane and Jamie were resting in their hotel room after a busy day in Washington and a Veteran's Day event. Diane said, "Jamie, I can't sleep, I'm worried about the bills due for the memorial so I'm going out to sit at the memorial and maybe this will give me some inspiration."

Jamie exclaimed, "It's not safe for you to go alone."

Diane said, "I'll be all right, don't worry about me." She sat at the memorial for awhile and then she saw a man walking around the Vietnam Memorial Wall and over to the round Women's Memorial. He just stood there staring at the statue and was very emotional. Diane walked over to him and said, "Here is a shoulder to lean on I'm a nurse." He said his name was Dick Del Rossi and he told her his story. She mentioned the memorial was in serious financial difficulty.

He said, "I think I have a solution to your problem, because my cousin owns theaters all across the country. I will call him and maybe he will have a solution."

Six weeks later Paul Del Rossi told her he would have a one-night benefit performance in 50 theaters across the United States. The revenue from that event would go toward the memorial's debt. The price was $10 for the movie, popcorn and a Pepsi. There were no big corporate or private donors - that was the theme. It was individuals making a contribution one night across America for this memorial, - titled *America Remembers* and the movie was *Air Force One* starring Harrison Ford.

They raised one million dollars and all of it went to eliminating the debt owed on the Vietnam Women's Memorial. At a meeting of the board, the loan documents on the memorial were burned on Memorial Day. This was quite a moment for Paul Del Rossi as well as the Women's Vietnam Memorial Committee. The committee soon appointed Paul to the Board.

Jamie was honored at this same meeting with a two thousand dollar painting of a nurse at the Vietnam Veteran's Wall given to her by Paul Del Rossi.

CHAPTER 21

The Morning of the 10th Anniversary

Paul Del Rossi had gone out to the Women's Vietnam Memorial with his cousin Dick at 6 a.m. on the occasion of the 10th anniversary of the dedication of the memorial to place a wreath at the memorial when there would be no one there and they could be alone in their thoughts. There was a young man standing there with a red rose. Paul walked up behind him and the young man asked if he knew if Evangeline Jamison was still alive. Del Rossi said she was alive and would be at the memorial later that day. He said "I knew her in Vietnam. I was brought in on a stretcher. I was only 19 years old and I knew I was going to die, and I told her I was going to die. She took my hand and said, "I won't let you die." He had ridden on his motorcycle all the way from Hyannisport, Massachusetts, so he could be there at dawn, when there wouldn't be anyone there. He came just to put the rose on the Vietnam Women's Memorial in honor of Jamie. Del Rossi asked for his name, but he said it didn't matter. "Well, there wouldn't have been anyone there, but my cousin and I came to place a wreath from the Fitzgibbon family at the Women's Memorial". kismet, I guess." What is significant about the Fitzgibbon story is they are the only known father and son on the Wall.

✧ ✧ ✧

10th Anniversary of the Vietnam Women's Memorial

In 2003, Jamie was at the Veteran's day reunion in Washington, D.C. at the 10th anniversary of the founding of the Vietnam Women's Memorial, she was accompanied by her niece, Esther. It was quite a reunion for Jamie also because her Vietnamese adopted daughter Jane met them there.

At the Vietnam Women's Memorial, group after group of men in the Rolling Thunder group came up and thanked Jamie for her support and her fellow nurses for their support in the war. They were thanking her and the other nurses for being there for them and their buddies.

Jamie was watching all of this and before she knew it, Artie Muller asked if she would like a ride on Trike, then he put one of his bandana scarves around her head, a helmet and one of their Rolling Thunder T-shirts on her. Then they wanted to take Jamie for a ride. Jamie thought they were kidding but explained because of her bad hip, she could not get her leg up high enough for a motorcycle seat. So he put her in a sidecar on the motorcycle. They took her to the head of the parade of motorcycle Vets riding around the Pentagon, across the bridge to D.C. past the Jefferson Memorial and Lincoln Memorial and the Capitol. When they delivered her back at the Vietnam Women's Memorial she said, "WOW! What a ride - I guess I had to reach the Big 80 to ride a motorcycle! I really can't believe I did this." Col. Jane Carson and Diane Evans were also taken on the bikes around the memorials.

✼ ✼ ✼

Rolling Thunder - the Run was started in 1987. Ray Manzo and Artie Muller both wanted to do something about the POW/MIA issue. They wanted to wake up the American public, and educate them about the many American POWs who had been left behind. They wanted to pressure the United States government to let them know they were not satisfied with their inaction on the POW/MIA issue. They wanted, as Artie says, "To shake the hell out of the United States government and expose the cover-up, lies and the corruption." Ray came up with the idea to do a motorcycle run for the issue. Rolling Thunder Ride for Freedom of all POW/MIAs was born.

Artie tells how Larry, Lefty, Greasy, Walt, John, Ted and a few others were in Rolling Thunder from the beginning. Ray and Artie worked on organizing veterans and supporters to the demonstration. They all worked hard trying to reach out to every corner of America to notify everyone about the American POWs abandoned after past wars. John Holland, Walt Sides and Ted Sampley worked on whatever they could to make this happen. They did it because they care about the freedom of their brothers abandoned in POW camps. The same government that sent them there to fight (The United States government) had no intention of winning. Many American Prisoners of War were abandoned and died in POW camps after WWII, Korea and Vietnam War.

Many brothers came to Rolling Thunder I from all over the United States. There were some 2,600 riders in Rolling Thunder I and thousands of brothers and sisters lined the streets as Rolling Thunder roared into Washington, D.C. To quote Artie, "It was one hell of a Run. One had to be there to feel the rush in his veins." Proud Vietnam Veterans numbering 2,600 plus at Rolling Thunder I grew to hundreds of thousands of brothers and sisters returning every year. The North Pentagon parking lot overflows every year and tens of thousands park in Washington, D.C. before the Run. Veterans, men, women and children line the Memorial Bridge.

Their purpose was and is to honor brothers and sisters on the Wall as well as Veterans of all wars who gave their lives for their country. They demonstrate to people worldwide POW/MIAs do exist. They demand a complete accounting of all POW/MIAs and insist on bringing home all live American POWs still held by communist countries. They protect our future Veterans so they will be guaranteed they will not be left behind. That is what Rolling Thunder is all about.

Artie says, "In the next war, police action, conflict or whatever our elected leaders get us into, let these politicians let their children fight in the Hell of war and we are sure to bring all the politician's kids home. Many brothers from all of the United States, Canada, Australia, England, South Korea, New Zealand, Germany and many other countries have helped us put these Runs together. Guys like Greasy, Rat, Bungee, Slick, Guardrail, Filthy Phil, Buzz and many others have helped make this one of the largest Runs for the POW/MIA issue worldwide." Artie's wife is his biggest supporter and has helped him from the beginning, giving him all her support and encouragement.

Hundreds of thousands of men, women and children attend Rolling Thunder in Washington, D.C. each year. They come to participate in the event from all around the world. If you love your freedom, be at Rolling Thunder and ride for the freedom and full accounting of all Prisoners of War/Missing in Action from all wars. Remember to pay your respects to all our brothers and sisters who gave their lives for their country. Remember, you don't have to ride a bike to be part of Rolling Thunder. If you don't ride, line the streets of Washington, D.C. and be part of the true American spirit. Be part of the hundreds of thousands of Veterans and supporters who line the streets in support of the POW/MIAs left behind. You have to care. Give up some time for those who can't speak for themselves. Protect future generations of Veterans. Pressure the United States government to account for the known POWs taken captive by enemy forces and never returned. Keep the faith and remember all POW/MIAs and family members.

☆ ☆ ☆

The Ceremonies

Before the 10th anniversary of the Vietnam Women's Memorial ceremonies began, 10,000 Americans, Australians and Canadian veterans marched down Constitution Avenue led by military and civilian Vietnam veterans while thousands of people shouted, "Welcome Home", and "Thank you, Ladies" just a few minutes before the Armed Services Band opened the ceremony.

During the program, all the speakers were introduced in front of the Vietnam Women's Memorial. Jamie was there in a wheel chair. Esther and Jane had her sitting to the side of the memorial so she'd be there for everybody. She received a standing ovation. Jamie managed to raise herself up elegantly from the wheel chair and acknowledge the cheers.

At 1:00 pm, the Ceremony at the Wall began. The prelude to the Ceremony at the Wall was presented by the Band of the Nation's Capitol, the 257th Army Band. They performed, Put a Little Love in Your Heart, a song written and sung by Jackie DeShannon.

Ronald Gibbs introduced himself as a Vietnam Veteran who served on the Board of Directors of the Vietnam Veterans Memorial Fund and welcomed everyone to this Veterans Day 2003 at the Vietnam Memorial Wall and the 10th anniversary of the Vietnam Women's Memorial. He mentioned Jan Scruggs, the founder of the wall who couldn't be present. "Jan Scruggs is the visionary and inspiration, leader and champion behind building the wall. This memorial is the most visited in the nations capital. It stands for honor, service and sacrifice of 58,000 men and women killed in Vietnam and for all those who served."

He then introduced Janis Nark. "The Mistress of Ceremonies is a retired Army Lt. Colonel who is a member of our Board of Directors who served in Vietnam and Desert Storm. Lt. Colonel Janis Nark." She welcomed everyone to the 22nd annual Veteran's Day observance at the Wall, and said, "This years ceremony is also the 10th anniversary of the Vietnam Women's Memorial." Lt. Colonel Nark introduced and welcomed Raymond F. Du Bois Jr., who is the Mayor of the Pentagon, Director of Administration and Management in the office of the Secretary of Defense, Deputy and Undersecretary of Defense for Installations and Environment and he is also a Vietnam Veteran. Colors were presented by the Armed Forces Color Guard. All remained standing while the colors were presented and were retired. They were joined on top of the wall by Ft. Hood's first Cavalry Division and 3rd Signal Brigade, Ft. Braggs 82nd Airborne Division, and flanking the stage was the 1st Wheelchair Honor Guard from the Paralyzed Veterans of Americas Lone Star Chapter of Dallas, Texas.

Vietnam veteran Lt. Wayne Manson (Ret.) sang our National Anthem. Next, Vietnam Vet Alan Bowers, National Commander of the Disabled Veterans led, the Pledge of Allegiance.

After a number of speeches, Lt. Colonel Nark then introduced Diane Carlson Evans. "Diane Carlson Evans is a former Army nurse, Vietnam veteran, the only woman in the history of America to spearhead a campaign to have a national monument placed in Washington D.C. The result after a 10-year effort, honors all women, military and civilian, who served during the Vietnam War.

Diane Carlson Evans said, "Soldiers home from Iraq, soldiers home from all around the world, everywhere you have served - welcome home! Thank you. On behalf of the Vietnam Women's Memorial Foundation, welcome to the 10th anniversary of the dedication of the Vietnam Women's Memorial, welcome veterans and friends too. We have friends here from all over the world, from our territories. Our brothers and sisters whose names are inscribed on the wall - I know they welcome us too. They speak to us here in silence and we to them in spirit and in our hearts. And now, I want to welcome our women veterans whom the Vietnam Women's Memorial honors and will stand forever. The monument stands portraying your service, your courage, your legacy to our nation. Special thanks to the grand lady of the Army Nurse Corps Lt. Colonel Evangeline Jamison in the wheelchair, a veteran of WWII, Korea, and Vietnam. Also Mary Edith Meeks, and Ann Cunningham, Richard Scultz and the dearest sweetest woman in the world, outside of Evangeline Jamison, Shirley Crowe, wife of Admiral Crowe. She served on our board for 10 years. And there is a very special person on the stage for the first time, he is usually invisible, my phantom person in my life who is a great man behind this woman, Dr. Michael Evans please stand. Seven years in the Army medical Corps operating on the wounded soldiers who came home from Vietnam. Today he operates at the Ft. Harrison Veterans Hospital in Helena, Montana. We are grateful to all of these people, all of those who have worked so hard to make a difference for veterans, for women veterans and our brother veterans, thank you to the Vets Center who have been here for days and will be here through this evening, for being on site, for being here to help and support and will be here this evening in our mission of healing and hope. Dr. Al Bosrus is one of the greatest people in our VA system and he is here with us. Thank you. Thank you to all our donors and sponsors. Without them we could not achieve our goals.

"We give special thanks to Rolling Thunder, Artie Muller, here on stage for not only being behind us but for being beside us all along the way; Rolling Thunder, we thank you. Representing all the thousands of families, Janis Nark has already introduced them but we can't say enough about them, the Gold star mothers, we love you, Gold star wives, Sons and Daughters. I want to thank you for letting me indulge for a few minutes in expressing gratitude but the bronze monument of three women and a wounded soldier did not just happen to fall out of the sky and land right there. It took years of persistence and unrelenting effort, but today we affirm that the women it represents and the wounded soldier it represents deserve lasting preeminence, long lasting historical significance. That was one of the things I had to prove at a hearing I attended. I had to prove that adding a memorial here would be of lasting preeminence and long lasting historical significance. I think we proved it. Now we move on. On Veterans Day ten years ago the Vietnam Women's project dedicated the beautiful monument honoring the thousands of women who served in Vietnam. The wounded soldier cast in bronze revealed the painful reality of war. The sister soldiers surrounding him revealed their courage, compassion and life saving measures.

"Today we are honored to have Dr. Elizabeth Norman speak about the women the monument represents. Dr. Norman is not a veteran but she is passionate about researching and writing about military women who served during wartime. The year of our dedication in 1993, she received a commendation from the Department of the Army for military research. She has also received accolades from the New Jersey Department of Veterans Affairs for research of nurses who served in the Vietnam War. She is a professor of a PhD program in New York University of Nursing. In 1990 she published her first book, which is titled, Women at War. She has written a second book, We Band of Angels. The untold story of American women trapped on Bataan by the Japanese. Her book has been reviewed by 60 major newspapers, and Associated Press International Newspapers. She is currently working on her third book titled, Tears in the Darkness. Dr. Norman served on the volunteer of New York state coordinators for the Vietnam Women's Memorial Project prior to the dedication of the monument. She was deeply committed to the recognition and honor of all women, military and civilian who served during the Vietnam War. She lives in Montclair, New Jersey. Please welcome Dr. Norman."

After thanking Diane Carlson Evans, the memorial committee, fellow citizens and Gold Star mothers and greeting the soldiers from Walter Reed, Dr. Norman said, "Twenty-one years ago, I was busy making phone calls to various military and civilian organizations to try to find a list of nurses who had served in Vietnam. Finally I asked the Lt Colonel at Walter Reed and he replied, "We never thought it was important to keep track of female nurses. We saw no need." I was astounded and I knew if no one thought about the nurses, other women must be more hidden if this was possible.

"There was a dilemma women faced when confronting patriotism and how to carry out this obligation to our country. Even after two world wars, traditionally women supported fighting men at home as wives, mothers, sisters and friends. Combat was a man's world. What could possibly be more masculine than fighting and living in foxholes, climbing into an aircraft loaded with bombs and sliding behind the ship's gun-battery. The fact that women can, (and had) survived, in war situations undermined this image. You challenged this perception, offered your skills and served.

"One woman who confronted this dilemma said, "As a female, I couldn't be drafted like a man but I felt I had an equal responsibility to my country. I had a need not only to support my country but my own age group, at the time when there was so little concern about the boys that were fighting in Vietnam." She worked in Da Nang for 12 months.

"You volunteered to serve in a military or civilian role and experienced a time in your life that remains unique, a focal point to which all other life experiences are compared. Nothing will ever be the same after what you witnessed. You saw the best and worst of humankind - courage and selflessness, cruelty and cowardice.

"As one woman said, 'You grow up fast. A piece of me got old in Vietnam, and I have been an old lady since Vietnam even though I was only 22 at the time.'

"You served your country when women were confined to narrow, military roles and few civilian opportunities. Some would argue that you did not experience the raw reality of war but to anyone who listens to your stories, that comment is simply not true. You came to know war intimately. Soldiers are often too occupied with the business of fighting and dying to keep the awful inventory of battle. Only later does the scope of the slaughter really begin to stagger them, but you saw the deaths and the maiming and the emotional devastation in a way no one else did.

"The monument we are celebrating illustrates your experiences and brings the anguish and ambiguity into sharp focus. I look at the standing figure of the woman and imagined her listening to the sound of helicopters. After a few months overseas how many of you could tell, without looking up, what type of helicopter was flying nearby and whether it was empty or full.

"The second woman kneeling at the monument could be holding a helmet of someone she knew. If there was one shared reward for your service, it was the camaraderie among those around you. As one woman said, 'My true brothers and sisters were the people I was with in Vietnam.' That empty helmet she holds could have belonged to her friend.

"I look at the third figure cradling a man and think of the rapid evacuation system that brought in the wounded that would have been lost in previous wars. A few of those wounded could not be saved - the expectant cases with a hopeless prognosis. All the nurse could do was squeeze the hand or whisper into the ear of these patients. But often you did more.

"When the end was near, said one nurse, 'I would just stand near him. I felt that his mother would feel better knowing that someone was with her son when he died.' That soldier represented every young man who went off to fight a war and never returned. The nurse is every woman who ever mourned the loss of a husband, son, a brother or a friend.

"Whether military or civilian, he came home from Vietnam with an underwhelming greeting. Never again will any of you be forgotten. You have this memorial to remind everyone of what you have done. Long after you are gone, this monument will speak for you.

"Since you first gave voice to women in patriotism and service, our mothers, our grandmothers, aunts, uncles and others have spoken, raised funds and had memorials built to their service as women veterans. One woman, who was a prisoner of the Japanese, said to me. 'Once the gals from Vietnam started talking, I, too, knew that I had something to say. Not all of it was nice, if I didn't tell my story and the lessons I had learned no one would know.'

"So every time you go home and see a memorial to women who served - you began it all. You also made an important contribution to our country. You supported others and you saved lives. By accomplishing this objective so successfully, you invested in the future, everyone's future, and there's not a greater gift that a woman can give. "As the daughter of two WWII war veterans, as the wife of a radioman who served with the Second Battalion 9th Marines, and in Vietnam in 1968, the mother of the son who recently returned from serving his country as a Peace Corps volunteer in Togo West Africa, I deeply thank you."

There was a resounding ovation at the end of her speech.

CHAPTER 22

After Hours

During the time Jamie was working on the memorial, she was on the TV program China Beach on Memorial Day and met Tyne Daly. Jamie spoke of how really glorified the television show actually was, a big difference from the way things really were.

Jamie was also on Good Morning America along with Diane Carlson Evans talking about the statue and raising money for the project. Jamie has been honored and has spoken at many military functions and has been written about in newspaper articles too numerous to mention. Jamie also has appeared on television during many Veteran's Day and Memorial Day ceremonies.

There were many Nurse Corps reunions. There was one in California Jamie planned. There were 30 former Army nurses on this occasion at Jamie's home for cocktails. They all stayed at a hotel in Walnut Creek and went to a winery on a bus to Livermore, had lunch and sat and talked over old times in the lobby.

The last reunion for the nurses was in Portland, Oregon. Jamie's dear friend Smitty was there also. They had gone to nursing school together and used to double date. She lived in Aurora, Colorado for many years with her husband Tom and her 3 kids. Jamie and Smitty had grown up a couple of miles from each other in Iowa, but they had only met in nursing school and then went overseas together.

Jamie took a trip to Hawaii with her old nurse friend Kay Meyer. She enjoyed taking hula lessons while there. She made several trips to San Antonio to see an old friend whom she met who was a POW in the Philippines and who lived in San Antonio. Jamie traveled extensively to many states visiting her nurse friends in Mexico, New Mexico and Arizona with other friends.

Jamie was accepted into the Officer's Wives Club in Rossmoor since she was a female officer. The club had always been reserved traditionally for membership of Military Wives only but Jamie was the exception.

It was a very sad day for Jamie when her brother Bert died in 1995. He was the dearest thing in her entire life. It was most traumatic for the family and especially for Jamie because he and his family had lived close to her for 20 years.

EPILOGUE

We'll Meet Again

Jamie made a trip to Brook General Hospital in San Antonio, Texas and met her old boyfriend Brad whom she had met so long ago in New Guinea. They had kept in touch over all the years and all the wars. Her first impression was he looked wiped out. He was the Medical Service Officer there. He came to the hotel where she was staying to pick her up to go dancing, and have dinner. She went to a lot of dances in her life and loved to dance ... but now she was in a wheelchair. The minute he saw her, his face lit up with that old familiar smile and his smile touched her so ... and she felt the love she still had for him that had lasted for all these years.

It was as if Brad and Jamie had seen each other only yesterday. He picked her very gently up out of her wheelchair and guided her to the dance floor and held her in his arms very tenderly. Jamie cried inside for all the love she could have had with him all those years. He looked at her with so much love in his eyes and she felt guilty of robbing him of her love. He had asked her to marry him long ago in New Guinea but she had chosen her dedication to saving lives. She said, "You asked me once if I would marry you and I have wondered all along if I did the right thing."

He answered, "You have been a mother to many men and women. What a totally unselfish life you have had. I'm so very proud of you for all you have done." He would always love her. He had loved her over the span of 40 years.

As he held her in his arms she said, "You know, I have always loved you. You will always be the love of my life. I never stopped loving you."

She had been married to the Army and her duty to the country. She had lots of opportunities to marry but there was just one very special person, and that was Brad.

After their last dance, to the music of *We'll Meet Again,* they kissed and he reluctantly took her home. As they stopped at the door of her hotel, he gave her one last kiss and then he turned and walked away, but when he got to the end of the sidewalk he turned around to face her and gave her a snappy salute and blew kisses to her with both hands. And then he was gone, never to see her again. It broke her heart to see him go but he would always be in her heart of hearts, always a part of her. She was so blessed to have been able to know him, to see him again, and see he was all right.

✡ ✡ ✡

As she tells me this last chapter of her life, though, she thinks about the life she could have had, a question forms in her mind and I can sense she has something important to say. "Bev, I did do the right thing."

✡ ✡ ✡

And the angels speak softly with comforting words of kindness, goodness and love, great love, – the highest form of love is love for your fellow man. Do you know what it is like to speak with an angel?

Jamie has been an instrument in the healing of so many. She was also the foundation and a mentor for those who would go after her. It is truly amazing after being in three wars and seeing the terrible destruction men have wrought against each other Jamie is not bitter. She has maintained her strong inimitable character intact and is still the loving, kind, and gentle soul she always was.

I once said to her, "You would get along with anybody, Jamie."

Jamie replied, "Why not, if they're God's children. They're mine too!"

How lucky all those wounded men, women and children were to have her in that place and time to help them. Jamie is a mother to the world.

Jamie said, "My happiest times were everywhere. These memories are with me every day."

I asked her if she was born under a lucky star, and this was why she wasn't hit by any stray bullets. I said, "You know, Jamie, I think that the good Lord had a hand in that."

Jamie said, "You mean God did? Oh, I hope so."

I replied, "I think He had a lot to do with your life Jamie. He has helped you all along the way."

Jamie replied, "I hope He loves me, I love Him." She thought about it a moment and said, "And there's not a puppy or a soldier that I don't love."

What a GREAT LADY! To know Jamie is to love her. Jamie is a symbol of all that is good about America. She will always live in the hearts of men and women whom she has known and served through the years.

If anyone ever asks if it's possible for one person to make a difference in this world, tell them all about Evangeline Jamison. She made a difference.

Now Jamie is retired and "Sitting on top of the world, where you can see forever from her deck." She is a much loved and revered lady. Everybody brought something different to her life. To quote Jamie, "It's been a GRAND OLD TIME."

To know Jamie is to love her.

Now you know her.

APPENDIX

Vietnam Women's Memorial Project

From the beginning, the VWMP has searched and tried to identify the 265,000 military and civilian women who served during the Vietnam War. They have identified 13,000 names of women the Project has received. This Project gives the women a voice. All of this has given these women pride in what they did because they are all heroes of our country. They had deep wounds and an indifferent public unreceptive to them after the war. Now they are coming out and speaking at schools and writing about their experiences and helping one another.

✿ ✿ ✿

Glenna Goodacre

At age 16, Glenna was already painting and was inspired by famous artists on a trip to Europe as mentioned in her book Glenna Goodacre: First 25 Years. She was a successful painter before she began sculpting. In 1969 she visited a local foundry and the owner gave her a little ball of wax and she did a tiny sculpture of her daughter Jill. The only tools she had were a nail and a hairpin. She continued to do both painting and sculpture, but eventually started doing three-dimensional work. She did her first life-size piece, a nude figure, in 1981 and things started getting bigger and bigger. She still paints for family members. In her large monumental works she is more interested in the mass and composition. The viewers love the narrative and are moved by it. She works on several pieces at once. Glenna's accomplishments since the dedication of the Vietnam Women's Memorial are the US Mint coin portrayal of Sacagawea the Shoshone Indian teenager who was interpreter for explorers Lewis and Clark on their westward trip. Glenna is a successful painter of portraits and Native American subjects. Her 7 1/2 foot standing portrait of Ronald Reagan stands at the Reagan Library in California. A copy of this same figure is at the National Cowboy and Western Heritage Museum in Oklahoma City. Goodacre has more than 50 other bronze portraits in public collections in the United States. Among them are sculptures of Dwight D. Eisenhower, Barbara Jordan, Katherine Anne Porter, Scott Joplin, Greer Garson, Dan Blocker and General Hap Arnold. Her most recent sculpture is the Irish Memorial commemorating the 150th Anniversary of the Great Hunger. This was dedicated in 2002. It is a monumental bronze which stands 12 feet high, 30 feet long, and 12 feet wide. Her best-known work is the Vietnam Women's Memorial.

✠ ✠ ✠

Carolyn Tanaka

Carolyn Tanaka was asked by Evangeline Jamison to serve the effort for the memorial on the development committee.

Carolyn, as a child, along with her family, had been forced to live in Japanese Internment camps during WWII in Arizona. When the war ended her father moved the family to Fresno. She graduated as Salutatorian of her High School class. She attended Fresno State where she received a 3-year scholarship to the Fresno General Hospital School of Nursing. She was Class President and Valedictorian.

All Carolyn's male relatives joined the service to prove their loyalty to the United States. Her brother joined the Air Force and her cousin Abraham Osama joined the famous 100th Infantry Batallion/442nd Regiment Combat Team. This was formed in Hawaii of Japanese Americans willing to give their lives to prove their loyalty to their country.

Since all of Carolyn's male relatives had joined the service, Carolyn thought it was her duty to serve her country also. Friends asked, "How could you join the military, you were treated so badly by your government. Why do you want to fight this senseless war in support of that government?" Her answer was, "I have a skill that is needed in Vietnam and I'm going there to serve my country."

Carolyn graduated from Fresno General Hospital School of Nursing. She joined the Army Nurse Corps in 1966 and was sent within months to Vietnam.

During that tour she was head nurse in the ER at the 24th Evacuation hospital in Long Binh. She had been awarded the Bronze Star Medal and decided to extend her tour of duty to 18 months.

"On returning home from Vietnam, coming into Oakland California, we were advised to get out of uniform to avoid being spat upon or called baby killers. We gave our blood, sweat, and tears for our brothers in combat and this was the thanks we got."

Carolyn has spoken for and very diligently raised funds for the Vietnam Women's Memorial. She was unpaid and paid her own expenses, postage for mailings, motel bills for overnight stays, etc. She worked tirelessly going up and down the state of California talking to packed assemblies. She was asked to be Grand Marshal for the Fresno Veteran's Day parade and guest speaker for the Pappy Boyington Memorial luncheon. Pappy Boyington was an ace pilot in WWII who lived in Fresno and had just passed away. She was the first female Grand Marshal in the 67-year history of this parade.

In 1994 Carolyn was inducted into the Legion of Valor Museum in Fresno founded in 1890 "to represent all women in all wars".

Arline, Carolyn's daughter, was reading the March 8, 1989 issue of People magazine, which had a story about Rory Bailey, a Vietnam veteran who lost his entire face from an exploding rocket. She asked, "Mom, isn't this the patient you took care of in Vietnam?" Sure enough it was. She contacted People Magazine and they put her in touch with Rory by phone. "It came with surprisingly great ease. He was so down to earth, so positive, we just carried on the best conversation. We talked for 45 minutes. In writing to People Magazine I asked if they would pay his way to Washington, DC and for us to meet at our memorial. I kept in touch with People Magazine and Rory through four years until the memorial was dedicated. Yes, People magazine was interested in doing a story on our reunion and would pay his way and also for whomever needed to accompany him.

The reporter Giovanna Breau went to the train depot to pick up Rory. When we got to the memorial Rory was standing in front of it. I went up and gave him a big hug. As we clung to one another, in silence, he uttered the words I was longing to hear, 'Thank you for being there.' That moment released all the feelings of guilt I had over so many years knowing he was still alive and going through all the reconstructive surgery. Col.

Jane Carson of VWMP was very gracious to unveil the memorial just for this interview. It was re-covered until Dedication Day.

"At the dedication I took Rory with me for the march down Constitution Avenue with the 24th Evac group. I took Rory by the hand and we pushed our way to the front of the memorial. We danced with the Native Americans in their dance."

Rory could not speak for 10 years. It is unimaginable how that must have been for him. He is now happy he can speak. She continues to include him in her trips and gatherings. Carolyn took Rory on a fishing trip. When he came back even though he was blind, he had caught the biggest fish on that trip. He now has learned to be a carpenter and also makes afghans he sells at trade fairs where he lives in Illinois.

✡ ✡ ✡

Wreaths Placed at the Vietnam Women's Memorial

Wreaths were placed at the memorial, by The Gold Star Mothers of America, Walk of the Warriors, Navajo Women's Vietnam Veterans, American Red Cross, Nine X Corporation, American Association of Nurse Anesthesists, Gold Star Wives of America, Military Order of Purple Heart, Chapter 63, Jewish War Vets, Viet Now National, Vietnam Veterans Association of Australia, Vietnam Veterans of Australia, Glendale Heights Junior Women, Fox Valley Chapter of Viet Now, Waterbery Area Vietnam Association, Vietnam Veterans of America Chapter 9, Vietnam Veterans of America Chapter 82, Vietnam Veterans of America, Chapter 97, Vietnam Veterans of America, Chapter 349, Vietnam Veterans of America Chapter 435, Vietnam Veterans of America Chapter 10, Vietnam Veterans of America Chapter 541, Veterans of Foreign Wars Illinois, Veterans of Foreign Wars Post 8081, Veterans Caucus, Navy Seabees Veterans of America, Vietnam Veterans of the State of New Jersey, Duster Quads Searchlights, Vietnam Veterans of America, Chapter 233, Inter Veterans Council of Saginaw County Illinois, American Nurses Association, Children's Medical Relief International, Rolling Thunder Pennsylvania, Tri-County Council Vietnam Era Veterans, Sharon Lane Memorial Chapter 199, Vietnam Veterans of America Chapter 649, Vietnam Veterans of America Montgomery County, Edward C. Seymour VFW Post #1231, and the Ladies of the Unit, Vietnam Veterans of America Chapter 73, Vietnam Veterans Memorial Post 796, Delaware Valley Vietnam Veterans, National Order of Trench Rats, Disabled American Veterans Chapter 18, America West Airlines Operation Ruddertbury, Local 292 UAW, 11th Armored Calvary, J.J.'s Marine Corp. Pub Lowell, Massachusetts, Veterans of Vietnam War Inc., Viet Veterans 266 of Philadelphia, Vietnam Veterans FDR Hospital, Vietnam Veterans Chapter 452, Veterans for Peace, National Association of Neo Natal Nurses, Vietnam Vets Chapter 210, VVA Chapter 590. Representing the National Park Service here today is Robert Stanton, Bobby Keith, and John Reynolds who laid a wreath at the memorial.

☆ ☆ ☆

Colonel Janis Nark

Colonel Nark is a retired Lieutenant Colonel who served in the Army for 26 years. Her assignments included both Vietnam and Desert Storm. She is a Registered Nurse, an educator recognized by the military as an expert in Nuclear, Chemical and Biological Warfare and a former ski instructor who actually has a double black (experts only) ski run in Aspen named for her Nark's Nook. Colonel Nark is a multi-published author with stories in many books including three versions of Chicken Soup for the Soul series, as well as seven books about Vietnam. Janis is a professional Motivational Speaker. Her passion is dealing with change and stress and her unforgettable message is "Change is Mandatory, Stress is Manageable and Misery is Optional." (TM).

☆ ☆ ☆

Lillian Goldie Dekker

Goldie who had met her husband Fred at Camp Robinson, Arkansas during boot training married him in 1944. She was at the point of debarkation at Pittsburg California but didn't go to Australia. Her fiancée had graduated from Yale in the ROTC. He was a 1st Lieutenant. He would be on the battleship Missouri during the signing of Japan's unconditional surrender at the end of the war, and when he came home he had a beautiful little boy. In the future, they had another son and both sons would serve very proudly in the Navy.

Laws passed through Rolling Thunder endeavors

Missing Service Personnel Act of 1997

A bill, that would guarantee missing servicemen or women could not arbitrarily be killed on paper by the U.S. government, without credible proof of death.

Bring Them Home Alive Act of 2000 S-484

The act provides for the granting of refugee status in the United States to nationals of certain foreign countries in which American Vietnam War POW/MIAs or American Korean War POW/MIAs may be present, if those nationals assist in returning POW/MIAs alive.

Displaying of POW/MIA Flag Over Federal Buildings and Military Facilities

A law requiring federal buildings, all Post Offices, the Vietnam and Korean memorials in Washington, DC, and military facilities, fly the POW/MIA flag on six national holidays.

POW/MIA Memorial Flag Act of 2001 S-1226

This bill requires the display of the POW/MIA Flag at the World War II Memorial, The Korean War Memorial and the Vietnam Veterans Memorial on any day in which the United States Flag is displayed.

Persian Gulf War POW/MIA Accountability Act of 2002 S-1339

This bill is to amend the Bring Them Home Alive Act of 2000 to provide an asylum program with regard to American Persian Gulf War POW/MIAs.

S.3421 PUBLIC LAW 109-461

To encourage the hiring of members and former members of the Armed Forces who were wounded in service and are facing a transition to civilian life.

H. Con. Res. 125

Support for the designation and goals of Hire a Veteran Week and encouraging the President to issue a proclamation supporting these goals.

Veteran-Owned Small Business Promotion Act of 2005 H.R. 3082

Requires 9 percent of procurement contracts entered into by the Dept. of Veterans Affairs be awarded to small business concerns owned by veterans.

Veteran's Housing Opportunity and Benefits Improvement Act of 2006 S. 1235

Legislation to amend Title 38, United States Code, to provide adaptive housing assistance to disabled veterans residing temporarily in housing owned by a family member and to make direct housing loans to Native American veterans; make modifications to the Advisory Committee on Veterans Employment and Training within the Dept. of Labor; provide Life and Health Insurance coverage to certain veterans and their family members; and for other purposes.

Respect for Fallen Heroes Act
H.R. 5037

Legislation to prohibit certain demonstrations at cemeteries, under the control of the National Cemetery Administration at the Arlington National Cemetery and for other purposes.

✿ ✿ ✿

Rolling Thunder has been instrumental in the passage and promotion of many other bills.

✡ ✡ ✡

Author, Beverly Thompson

Beverly Thompson is a woman with first hand experience on the wards of an Army hospital in Japan during the Vietnam War as a Red Cross volunteer. Weekly she spent many hours with the worst wounded soldiers who were sent to this hospital from the Evacuation Hospitals like Evangeline Jamison's 93rd Evacuation Hospital in Vietnam during that war. Beverly is empathetic and knows what these men went through in the war. Patriotism and honor are of utmost importance to Beverly. She brings to the public a compassionate and heartwarming story about a Lieutenant Colonel Army nurse who is in a class with Amelia Earhart.

Beverly's knowledge of Japan and the Philippines is from real life. She lived in both countries and traveled extensively in these countries over a period of four years. She lived on the economy in Japan and became a part of that community.

She was a proofreader for a large newspaper, reading copy for four different in-house newspapers and typed live broadcast news on television for many years. She was Vice President of many art groups and Naval Officer's wives groups. She was a Naval Officer's wife for 23 years and the founder of a writers group in the San Francisco area in California.

Aside from being a writer she is an accomplished Illustrator/artist. Beverly received her degree in Illustration from California College of the Arts in California. She attended Chouinard Art School in California of

Walt Disney fame. The school is now California Institute of the Arts. She has worked with many large corporations who have bought her corporate logos or artwork. She has exhibited her paintings in Carmel, California and is currently exhibiting in several galleries in Texas. Being naturally insightful, her brushstrokes have truly turned into very descriptive words.

Beverly brings the Vietnam War up front and center. She knows the military ways, and what went on in the hospitals of that era.

This is an authentic story. The character building events that formed Jamie's life are woven into the fabric of her life and the uniform she wore and the service to her country are evidently clear.

Made in the USA
Lexington, KY
05 September 2012